Star of India

The Life and Films of Sabu

by Philip Leibfried

Published in the USA by:
BearManor Media
P O Box 71426
Albany, Georgia 31708
www.bearmanormedia.com

Printed in the United States of America
ISBN 978-1-59393-603-7

Book and cover design by Darlene Swanson • www.van-garde.com

Contents:

Dedicated to Jasmine Sabu,
she of the Babylonian eyes and gentle spirit,
who graced this earth for all too short a time.

Acknowledgements

A non-fiction book, like a motion picture, is a collaborative effort. No matter how much information the author has on his subject, he must still rely on the knowledge and experience of others for that extra input necessary for the most complete account possible. Such was the case with *Star of India*.

Much of the information concerning Sabu's last fifteen years would have been impossible to discover had it not been for the wonderful cooperation of Mrs. Marilyn Sabu, who was there that entire period. Besides the numerous letters she wrote in answer to my unending barrage of questions, she welcomed me as her guest one unforgettable afternoon in April of 1993. Patient and ever-smiling, she spoke warmly of her days with Sabu, proudly showing off mementos of his career, among them the knives he carried in *The Thief of Bagdad* and *Jungle Book*. To top it off, she fed me a wonderful seafood salad for lunch. I left her home with a full stomach, but with the distinct feeling that I had really missed something by not having had the opportunity to meet the subject of my book.

Many thanks also go to Madeline Matz, former Reference Librarian of the Motion Picture, Broadcasting and Recorded Sound Division of the Library of Congress, for her marvelous enthusiasm in assisting me. She, too, survived a seemingly unending series of questions and requests, digging relentlessly through mountains of material in the deepest abysses of the Library to provide me with answers to my often obscure queries.

Eternal gratitude is due to my oldest friend, Fred Yannantuono, who presented me with the gift of a word processor and printer, without which this project would undoubtedly still be in the works. Two late friends are also to be remembered for their contributions: the great British film director Michael Powell, who put me in touch with Marilyn Sabu back when I began my career article on Sabu and spoke of his days directing *The Thief of Bagdad*, and Bill Feret, who generously contributed time, information and material. Thanks also to Sabu's first American friend, Bud Knight, who welcomed me into his home for an interview, and who continued to help afterwards.

Much gratitude is due my friends Thom Sciacca and John Cocchi, who supplied me with videos of Sabu films and background information on them, as well as to the late Guy deVille, who shared important data on Maria Montez from his proposed book on her life and career. To Aurelia Antonucci, a sincere "Grazzi assai!" for her invaluable assistance in translating the technical credits for Sabu's two Italian films.

Special thanks also to Jasmine Sabu for contributing the introduction to the book, and for her moral support. I am very sorry that she did not get to see the finished book.

To Rudy Behlmer and his wife Stacey go many thanks for verifying certain data regarding Sabu's films. Unending gratitude is due my good friend, stuntman-turned-author Teel James Glenn, for his boundless support and for discovering some obscure photos.

Among Sabu's colleagues who took the time to answer my letters, the late Rosemary DeCamp stands out for her enthusiasm for the project, and for her contribution of a copy of her wonderful autobiography, *Tales from Hollywood*. Many thanks are also due to Mr. and Mrs. Osmond Borradaile, and the late Peter Ellenshaw, who assisted in the final solution of "the magic pebbles" mystery from *The Thief of Bagdad*. To the late Desmond Tester I am deeply grateful for taking the time to write two very informative and interesting letters about his days with Sabu and his own subsequent career. Much gratitude is due to the late Robert Kendall, whose own acting career was realized because of his resemblance to Sabu. To Cleo Laine, the late Valerie Hobson, the late Robert Douglas and the late Robert Stack go my warmest thanks for sending their memories of working with Sabu.

Heartfelt thanks to Madeleine Kaye of The National Film and Sound Archive of Australia for tracking down Desmond Tester for me. My deepest gratitude to Pat W. Battle for her contribution of many newspaper clippings and candid stills of Sabu. Sincere thanks to Marc Wanamaker, of Bison Productions, preserver of so much of Hollywood's heritage, for contributing rare stills and obscure information. Many thanks to Martin Stockham for his assistance, and for producing a fine documentary on Sabu for Great Britain's Channel Four, as well as for his beautiful book, *The Korda Collection*, both of which proved very useful. A hearty "Danke schoen!" to Willi Johanns of the Goethe Institute in Munich for his cheerful assistance with data on Sabu's German film.

My unending thanks to the following residents of Beaconsfield and its environs for their assistance regarding Sabu's school days: Miss A. K. Day, Dennis Mail, Julian Hunt, the Local Studies Librarian of the County Reference Library of Aylesbury, Bucking- hamshire and Martin Roundell Greene, principal of Merrion House, Beaconsfield, Buckingham- shire. To Lydia Girard goes much gratitude for loaning me two videos from her collection totally on trust, after I heard about her interest in Sabu from a mutual friend and wrote to her out of the blue. Many thanks to Jeff Heise for his patience in chauffeuring me around the Los Angeles area while I was out there.

My sincere gratitude to Jack Coogan of the Flaherty Center at the School of Theology at Claremont (Cal.) for providing me with a transcript of the radio program *Portrait of Robert Flaherty*. Sincere thanks to David Marowitz for providing material.

Thanks also to all of the following for responding to my author's query with reminiscences of their relationships with Sabu: Mrs. Donald H. Battin, the late Monroe Benton, Ardelle Brebner, Philip Castanza, Capitola Kean Murphy, Edward Tufte and Lynne Lehrman Weiner. To my very good friends and fellow film buffs, Annette D'Agostino Lloyd and Jim Low, much gratitude for your continued moral support. Special thanks to my good friend, the late Gene Vazzana, editor of *The Silent Film Annual*, for proofreading my rough draft. For their assistance with important details, Barry Hunt and Billy H. Doyle receive special mention.

Special thanks go to Alfred A. Knopf, Inc. for permission to quote from *A Life in Movies* (1987) by Michael Powell, and to Cambria Publishing for permission to quote from *Tales from Hollywood* (1989) by Rosemary DeCamp.

And last, but far from least, my eternal gratitude to Malcolm Willits, Sabu's greatest fan, who got the ball rolling for his long-cherished dream of producing a book on the career of his favorite film star after seeing my career articles on Sabu in *Filmfax* and *Films in Review*. His generosity, patience and encouragement, as well as his assistance in supplying material and data, made my task even more enjoyable.

PHILIP LEIBFRIED
New York, NY 2010

Introduction

"Your father was my hero! When I was a boy I wanted to grow up just like Sabu!"

All of my life I've heard these and similar sentiments expressed about my father, Sabu. A wonderfully refreshing actor, a war hero and a loving father - no daughter could be more proud of the man and the memory than I. Although our time together passed all too quickly, Sabu had an amazing impact on my life, my thoughts and perceptions, my spiritual and moral beliefs and my imagination which has led to my own career as a fantasy writer. I remember his quiet strength, trusting heart and giving nature. I have no hidden Hollywood horror stories to tell. I have only the impressions of a bigger-than-life man seen through the eyes of his adoring daughter.

Through my teenage years and my adult life it has been truly inspirational to learn of the still dedicated fans, both young and old, who tell me of my father's influence upon their own lives. Although swept from this earth at the young age of 39, Sabu's memory lives on through films that have been renovated and restored to their original masterful beauty and are played around the world to revive the faded memories of some and create new worlds of excitement for others. Through the painstaking work of skillful historians like Philip Leibfried and Malcolm Willits, the great times of Sabu's film career are now preserved in a delightful and informative collection of photographs spanning the years from his discovery through his short, but tremendously influential, career. Many thanks to Philip and Malcolm from my mother, Marilyn, my brother, Paul, and of course, myself for publishing this moving tribute to the life of Sabu.

"Wood and water; wind and tree. Jungle favor go with thee."

— JASMINE SABU

Chapter One
The Eyes Of Youth

India! The very name conjures up images as varied as its many languages – prowling tigers, golden temples, lush green jungles, the Taj Mahal gleaming jewel-like in the midday sun. A land of mystery and contradiction to western eyes, how must it have appeared in 1935 to an eleven-year-old boy whose world it was?

That year the people of the Asian sub-continent were still deeply embroiled in a political struggle for independence from Great Britain begun many years earlier. The country had not really been their own since the East India Company of England had commenced trading operations in Surat on India's northwest coast in 1612. The company continued to acquire land until it had footholds in several cities across the northern part of the country. The inevitable military influx followed when Robert Clive, second in command of East India Company forces, broke company policy and took the rich province of Bengal by force of arms in 1757. The centuries-old Mogul rule was thus effectively ended. Their mighty empire had been crumbling for years, due to a series of invasions and revolts which had drained their vast resources, and this latest intrusion was the straw that broke the elephant's back. The British began setting up protectorates around the country and by the third decade of the nineteenth century, the British *Raj* – the Hindu word for "rule" - was firmly established. Now, almost two hundred years after the collapse of the Moguls, Britain's Parliament passed the Government of India Act, the first step in the transfer of power to a federal structure run entirely by Indians. The days of "the white man's burden" were fast coming to an end.

Such events were of no concern to the youngster, for he lived far away from it all in Mysore, one of India's southernmost states. Although the site of four wars with the British in the latter half of the eighteenth century, things there were quiet now, so that the boy remained undisturbed in his universe, which consisted of his elephant and his friends at the royal elephant stables of the Maharajah of Mysore. Recently, however, his attention had been diverted by the arrival of a film crew from far-off England. Having heard that the white *sahibs* were seeking a boy to ride an elephant in their motion picture, he began hanging about while they shot background footage. Although he had never seen a motion picture, nor even knew what one was, the youngster yearned to be the one selected to ride the elephant for the movie men. The boy was certain that he could not fail to please the foreigners if given a chance to demonstrate his innate ability in handling the huge beasts. Little did the lad know, as he observed the film crew, that once given that opportunity, his life would be changed forever.

Who was this ambitious and confident young fellow?

His name was Selar Shaik. He had entered the world amidst the exotic flora and fauna of the Karapore jungle on January 27, 1924. His father, Ibrahim, a devout Muslim, was a mahout who doubled as a veterinarian in the employ of the Maharajah of Mysore. He became the sole protector of Selar and Dastagir, the boy's older brother by twelve years, when his wife, Zinabee, died a few years after giving birth to their second son.

Zinabee's people were originally from Assam, the extreme northeastern state of India, which had been settled by Mongols centuries before, so that Selar's lineage thus gained a trace of warrior blood. Ibrahim proved to be a fine teacher as well as a father. Early on he brought his younger offspring into contact with the gentle gray giants which were to figure so prominently in the child's future by teaching his elephant to rock the infant's cradle as he slept. At the age of three, little Selar rode atop the massive head of the pachyderm for the first time. A year later, the boy was taught how to swim. He undoubtedly acquired that skill in very short order, for the rivers of the

Karapur jungle are infested with crocodiles. Some time afterward, he related a close call he had with one rather large specimen. The reptile chased him onto a rock in the middle of a river, paused, then continued on its way, leaving film fans forever in its debt.

Naturally, Selar's ambition was to become a great *mahout*. He was very attentive to the maharajah's elephant drivers, watching them closely as they prodded and shouted commands at their towering charges. By the time he was seven the boy had become master of his father's elephant. That year, however, his education was halted when Ibrahim suddenly passed away. His *hathi* grieved, as tame elephants are wont to do when their masters die. Its grief was so great that it would neither eat nor obey commands, so Selar had no choice but to let the beast return to the jungle. With Dastagir now on his own driving a taxi on the wide streets of Mysore City, a trading, manufacturing and processing center for textile, rice and oil, Selar was made a ward of the maharajah.

With a pension of two rupees a month (then approximately seventy-five cents American), Selar loitered about the royal elephant stables under the watchful eye of the chief *mahout*. Perhaps as a means of ridding himself of some responsibility, that worthy thought it best to send the lad to school in Mysore City. A few boring, elephant-less days there were enough to send Selar fleeing to his uncle's hut in the jungle. His kinsman took him in, but tried his best to frighten the boy into returning to school with tales of man-eating tigers and evil jungle spirits. Nothing daunted the determined child, however; he merely added the stories to his increasing stock of jungle lore. Finally, his uncle took Selar by the hand and personally brought him back to the school.

This time the boy remained, but most of his free time was still spent back at the royal stables. There he took a special interest in a particular pachyderm named Irawatha, a monolithic creature that was by far the largest and strongest tusker in all of Mysore. The two formed a bond almost immediately, and soon they were inseparable. The youngster taught the huge animal many tricks, including having Irawatha curl its trunk around him and lift him onto its broad head. That was some ride for a little boy, considering the fact that the creature stood nine feet, eight inches tall at the shoulder.

Truly Ganesha, the elephant-headed Hindu god of good luck, smiled upon Selar, even though he was a Muslim. In any case, the partnership which was to culminate in a radical transformation of the fortunes of young Selar Shaik had begun.

Chapter Two
Elephant Boy

In June 1922, the first film to garner public interest for the yet-unnamed documentary genre was released. *Nanook of the North* depicted the everyday struggle for existence of an Eskimo hunter; its detailed narrative style was a revelation to audiences everywhere. Critics worldwide thumbed through their thesauruses in search of words worthy to describe this cinematic marvel. A financial success everywhere except in the United States, it was the creation of a thirty-eight-year-old American named Robert Flaherty.

Born in Iron City, Michigan, on February 16, 1884, Flaherty's earliest lessons had been learned at the school of life. As a youngster he had once spent two years with his father in a log cabin in Ontario, Canada, learning woodcraft from the local Native American tribes, an experience which formed the basis of his life-long interest in primitive cultures. *Nanook's* foreign box-office returns attracted the attention of producers in Hollywood, and soon Robert was accepting offers to conceive similar films. For Famous Players-Lasky he made the poetically didactic *Moana* (1926) in Samoa, but the parent studio, Paramount, failed to properly promote the picture; even though critically acclaimed, it fared poorly at the box office. Subsequent deals ended more unhappily as the studios insisted on meddling with Flaherty's style. After walking off two productions, he traveled to the British Isles, where he spent three years filming *Man of Aran*, a depiction of shark hunting in the vast loneliness of the Irish Sea. Released in 1934, it, too, was a commercial failure.

The following year, finding himself seriously in need of funds, the filmmaker recalled a brief meeting he had had in Hollywood in 1929 with a director named Alexander Korda. He approached the Hungarian émigré, who was now the head of London Films, Britain's most successful studio, with an idea for a film. Inspired by an incident he had witnessed while in Mexico in 1928, he had already co-written the story with his wife, Frances. Called "Bonito the Bull", it told of the friendship between a young boy and a fighting bull.

Korda, like Flaherty, was a nomadic type. Born Sandor Kellner, in 1893 near Turkeve, Hungary, he spent a decade directing films in his native country, as well as in Austria and Germany. Following three years in Hollywood and brief stints in Berlin and Paris, he finally settled in Great Britain in 1931, where he founded London Film

Productions Ltd. Two years later he had an international box-office hit with *The Private Life of Henry VIII* and found himself hailed as the savior of the theretofore moribund British film industry. He proved receptive to Flaherty's idea at their meeting, but remembering a similar story from the first of Rudyard Kipling's *The Jungle Books*, decided to alter the setting from Mexico to India and change the bull to an elephant. He offered to obtain the rights to the character, title and story of Toomai of the Elephants for use in Flaherty's proposed project. However, he made sure to word their contract so that he had control over the final phases of production. The American filmmaker agreed to the terms, Rudyard Kipling became some 5,000 pounds richer, and *Elephant Boy*, as the picture came to be known, was now in pre-production.

As preparation for this involved project, Korda had Flaherty hold some script conferences with Lajos Biro (1880-1948), a well-known Hungarian playwright-novelist who was then the script editor at London Films. As a young journalist, Korda had interviewed Biro some twenty years earlier in Budapest and through frequent contact they had become good friends, culminating in their very fortunate association at London Films.

Thus, it was in February of 1935 that Robert Flaherty found himself en route to Bombay, India, ironically, the birthplace of Kipling. His brother David had gone on ahead with a production manager to pave the way. They scouted several possible locations, among them the province of Mysore. When Robert arrived in early March, he journeyed to the north of India in search of a suitable site on which to film. While there, he received a telegram from the prime minister of Mysore in southern India, stating that the maharaja would be most pleased if the filmmaker would shoot *Elephant Boy* in his province. Since he was offered several enticing incentives, including the loan of an unused palace and animals from the Royal Zoo, Flaherty gladly accepted the ruler's invitation.

After cleaning out the cobras in the hunting palace loaned to him by the maharaja, the director was faced with having to work with a cameraman, whereas he had usually performed this task himself. In thirty-seven-year-old Osmond H. Borradaile (1898-1999) he found a spirit in accord with his own. Borradaile, a Canadian who had worked for ten years at Paramount as Lab Technician, Assistant Cameraman, and, finally, Operating Cameraman, had journeyed to England in 1930 and found work with London Films the following year. Having proven his worth by shooting the exteriors for such productions as *The Private Life of Henry VIII* (1933) and *Sanders of the River* (1935), it was felt that he was eminently worthy of lensing *Elephant Boy*.

As might be imagined, film processing methods were a bit primitive in southern India at that time. A staff of developers, inexperienced save for one man, had to labor in a building lacking air conditioning and a filtered water supply. Finding the situation intolerable, the lone experienced processor soon quit. He was replaced by an Indian who had once worked in a European laboratory. All the film was developed in shallow tanks, without machinery; only the soundtrack was sent to Bombay for processing.

Always a deliberate worker, Flaherty was further delayed by the arrival of the monsoon season in June. Lasting through early September, the inclement weather became cause for concern back in London. Six months had passed and Korda had received no footage. The original financing was for only twelve months. The only word the producer regularly received was from his business manager, who wrote to request additional funds.

Deciding to take action, Korda hired Hollywood director Monta Bell (1891-1958) as an assistant for Flaherty. Bell had worked for Warner Bros. and Metro-Goldwyn-Mayer in the 1920s, and was later production head at Paramount's Astoria, New York, sound studios. Unfortunately, his appearance at the site actually exacerbated matters. Bell had read a current novel entitled *Siamese White*, about a "ghost" elephant, and he thought this would provide a good subplot for *Elephant Boy*. Convincing Korda of this, Bell began using some of the book's elements. Considerable footage was shot before Flaherty got his hands on a copy of the book. Discovering that the "ghost" was really a white-washed pachyderm, and the "white" of the title just a man of that name, he was totally miffed. Korda was immediately informed of the wasted time and film, and Bell's footage was scrapped. Alex then sent his brother Zoltan (1895-1961) to oversee both Flaherty and Bell.

One of Alex's two younger brothers, Zoltan had been working for his older sibling since the latter's early days in Hollywood. A lover of exotica, he was pleased to be sent to India. So it was in the spring of 1936 that three different units were filming the Kipling tale, reportedly from three different scripts.

Meanwhile, Flaherty and Borradaile had been searching far and wide for the right boy to portray Toomai, and it is the cameraman who gets the credit for discovering little Selar Shaik. Intrigued by the handsome lad whom he saw giving an elephant a dressing down, he had the youngster tested. After several tests, the North Americans were happily satisfied that here was a real-life "Toomai of the Elephants". In fact, they were bowled over. Here was the answer to their prayers - right in front of them. They had found the real thing, in the real place. The precocious eleven-year-old could have told them as much, were he able to speak English then, or had the movie men been familiar with Urdu. As it was, his amazing ability in handling elephants, fine physique, and ingratiating naturalness before the camera did his talking for him. All the other boys who had been under consideration for the part were dismissed.

So the orphan boy now had a replacement "family"

- the members of the production unit of Elephant Boy. His confidence and curiosity were the talk of the camp, a camp which he happily kept in working order by doing every menial task that existed.

When the unit moved to a new location, the assistant director, Geoffrey Boothby, became worried about the boy. He asked Selar if he might become homesick; the plucky youth replied that he feared nothing and wished only to serve the white *sahibs*. Having also found an ideal figure to portray Petersen, the British government representative, in the person of a local coffee planter and hunter named Capt. Fremlin, the company was ready to get down to serious work.

Once real filming began, it was attended by the anxious moments which always seem to plague location shooting. One such episode occurred when a shot of an elephant crossing a turbulent river was needed. There were many volunteers, but none could get his elephant to enter the rapid current. Finally, Selar made Osmond Borradaile understand that his tusker, Irawatha, could ford the river. The cameraman had to be convinced by the head mahout to let the boy ride behind an adult *mahout* during the attempt. A stout cord was tied around Irawatha's neck for a handhold should either the mahout or Selar be swept off the beast's back. All went well until they were halfway across the raging river, when the current dragged even the mighty animal off its feet. The passengers were now struggling in the wild water, holding on for dear life. More than once the boy lost his grip, but each time managed to grab the rope again. Half a mile downstream the water was shallower, and the small party was able to make it safely to shore. His brave attempt netted the part of Kala Nag, Toomai's great tusker, for Irawatha. Selar was delighted to be working with his own elephant in the film. Unfortunately, that river scene did not survive the final cut.

Another incident concerned a shot wherein Kala Nag, carrying Toomai through a village, encounters an infant lying in its path. Toomai guides him carefully over the baby. When the child began crying, it was feared the pachyderm had accidentally stepped on it. Rushing the baby to the nearest doctor, it was discovered to be unharmed. The elephant had actually felt the child beneath its foot and shifted its weight so that the infant felt very little pressure. In the film, the toddler utters nary a whimper as Kala Nag steps cautiously over it, in a scene that brought gasps of disbelief from audiences.

Shortly after Flaherty began directing Selar's scenes, an unforeseen circumstance occurred. Irawatha began acting irrationally and attacked another elephant while the unit was en route to a location. A white spot appeared on the side of his head, a symptom of the temporary madness, or *musth*, which can strike an elephant without warning. Since for safety reasons the beast had to be chained, a substitute was used until he recovered. Only little Selar was able to approach him during that period, which fortunately ceased in time for Irawatha to appear in the filming of the *keddah*, or wild elephant roundup, one of the film's climactic scenes.

As a rule, *keddahs* were held only for visiting royalty or the arrival of a new viceroy, so lengthy preparations had to be made in the case of the film production unit. Eighty wild elephants were captured, herded into a specially built wooden stockade, and released only after filming was completed. The traditional *keddah* medal for the beaters was struck, this time designed by Flaherty himself. On one side was Selar atop Irawatha, on the reverse a camera and tripod.

The remainder of the shooting went quite well; Selar's older brother, Dastagir, was even given a bit part. Zoltan Korda was so impressed with Selar's talent that he changed the original script so that the young discovery had more screen time. Earlier, when Zoltan told brother Alex of his find, the renowned producer had been thrilled at the news. He immediately started thinking of a way to market his latest "commodity". Feeling that a single name would add to the boy's exotic appeal, Alex came up with "Sabu" as an identity for his new protégé. And "Sabu" it was, one of the few times in motion picture history a star became known by a single name.

Zoltan was not the only one impressed by the Indian youngster. Flaherty's wife, Frances, wrote much of him in her book *Elephant Dance*, which was published in 1937.

She particularly noted the amazingly close parallel between Sabu's life and that of the boy hero of "Bonito the Bull." A.K. Sett, honorary personal assistant to the prime minister of Mysore, recalled his first meeting with Sabu in a letter to Paul Rotha, one of Flaherty's biographers, in 1958: "My most treasured memory of this day is of Sabu... he made his appearance slowly, astride an elephant, and there he stood in the middle of the large compound for all to see him. Very thin and naked save for a small *lungi* round his legs and his head tightly covered with a white turban in the typical southern way... The manner in which he handled the ponderous, lumbering elephant was enough to stir one's confidence in him." Later in the same letter, he stated: "Years later, Sabu dined with me informally and alone....I told him how and where I first saw him.... This time he did not make his appearance on an elephant. He arrived in a luxurious Cadillac. He was most elegantly clad, not in a tight turban and skimpy lungi can assure you. And he spoke with a distinct American accent."

When all three units were recalled to London in June of 1936 for additional filming, Selar Shaik, with all the enthusiasm and curiosity of youth, went with them. He was accompanied by his older brother Dastagir, his pet mongoose (in case he encountered any cobras in the British countryside), and his *bulbul tharang*, a harp-like instrument he was fond of playing.

While passing through customs in England, Dastagir's

name was mistakenly entered as the family name. This error was never corrected, resulting in the use of "Dastagir" as the brothers' legal last name for the rest of their lives. "Shaik" now became the older brother's given name. The two of them were installed in a luxurious flat in London's West End while the finishing touches were put on *Elephant Boy*. Flaherty, who relied on editing to shape his films, had shot 300,000 feet of film without a cohesive plot. Alexander Korda could not wait for such a time-consuming operation to be completed, so using his power as stipulated in the contract, he hired the noted writer John Collier to create a storyline that would mesh with Flaherty's footage and which could be feasibly shot on the studio lot. Collier was a well-known author whose 1930 novel, *His Monkey Wife*, had raised some eyebrows. The tale of conjugal love between a man and a chimpanzee, it became his best-known work. He later emigrated to the United States, where he excelled in short stories and worked on many screenplays, including *Deception* (1946) and *The African Queen* (1951). He died in 1980. Collier, who had worked on only one film before, RKO's *Sylvia Scarlett* (1936), managed to devise a workable scenario for *Elephant Boy*. Zoltan then used the facilities of Alex's newly-finished complex known as Denham Studios to complete the filming. This took another six weeks. Included among his scenes was "the dance of the elephants" for which some tame pachyderms from a local zoo were used, along with several sets of rubber "el-

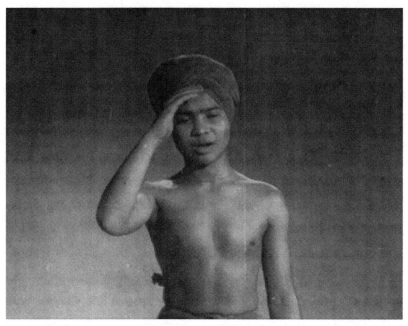

Elephant Boy (London Films, 1937) Sabu in the prologue

ephant feet". The latter were cleverly integrated with the shots of the live elephants.

Collier's script called for additional scenes for Petersen, so Fremlin's footage was jettisoned, much to Flaherty's annoyance, and probably Fremlin's as well. Replacing the hunter was actor Walter Hudd (1897-1963), a lanky gentleman who was the original choice for the lead in Korda's unrealized film on the life of T. E. Lawrence. A prologue was written for young Sabu in order to give him even more screen time and show off his rapid progress in learning English. For the scenes shot in India, the boy had pronounced his lines phonetically.

As soon as Sabu arrived in Britain, Alexander Korda began preparing him for his new life. He enrolled him in a school where he began his formal education. Sabu also had the run of the studio, a privilege made even more exciting by Zoltan Korda's gift of a midget auto which the fledgling actor exulted in driving around the lot.

Korda's feeling toward the young *émigré* became paternal, and at one point he attempted to adopt Sabu. His application was rejected by the British Government, perhaps due either to Sabu's alien status or Korda's being divorced. Contrary to many reports, the young Indian actor was never a ward of the British government. With that issue settled, the energetic and by-now-world-famous producer turned his attention to the more mundane matter of promoting the motion picture and the star upon which so many of his hopes rested.

Chapter Three
England and Fame

In the fall of 1936 Sabu had been enrolled at a school in Beaconsfield, a small suburb of a few thousand souls situated some twenty miles northwest of London, where he was now living with cameraman Osmond Borradaile and his wife, Christiane. The school, known as Beaconstone, was actually the home of its headmaster, a Merchant Service veteran named Thomas Thompson, who specialized in teaching the English language to youths who had the misfortune of being born in foreign lands. It was efficiently run by Capt. Thompson, who happened to be fluent in Urdu, Sabu's native tongue. The two got along swimmingly, especially after the young Indian mischievously tipped the sailboat on which they were riding one day, causing the good captain to fall overboard.

Halfway through the spring 1937 semester, *Elephant Boy* had its long-awaited premiere. So it was on the evening of April 7 that the former apprentice *mahout* found himself on the stage of the Leicester Square Theatre in London, salaaming and bowing as he received the warm applause of the audience which had been the first to view the highly-touted film. Billed as "The Picture with a Thousand Elephants and a Million Thrills!", *Elephant Boy* went on to do excellent business, more than justifying its 90,000 pounds ($450,000) cost.

The film is quite faithful to its inspiration. An uncomplicated picture, *Elephant Boy* tells of an Indian boy named Toomai who yearns to become a hunter like his father. He is already master of an elephant, and with persistence and great charm, manages to get the British governmental representative to allow him to join an elephant hunt. Initially mocked by the adult hunters for believing in the myth of "the elephants' dance", Toomai later witnesses just such an event. He leads the Briton and the hunters to the great herd of pachyderms, which are then driven into a corral specially constructed to hold them. He is named "Toomai of the Elephants" by the chief hunter and apparently makes his career move. The addition of a *mahout* who abuses Kala Nag, and having Toomai accompany Petersen to show him the wild elephant herd rather than remaining asleep in camp, are two of several minor differences between the source and the adaptation. No Kipling aficionado can quibble over these, as the film taken as a whole succeeds both as entertainment and literature-into-film. In fact, *Elephant Boy* was wholeheartedly endorsed by The Kipling Society of England (Kipling himself had died in January 1936), whose members were undoubtedly most pleased by the use of the author's very words in several scenes. Two instances are when Toomai brings Kala Nag to be inspected by Petersen, and the speech given by the great hunter Machua Appa when he renames the boy "Toomai of the Elephants".

According to film historian Rudy Behlmer, author of *Memo from David O. Selznick, Inside Warner Bros. (1935-1951)*, and *Behind The Scenes, The Making of...*, the success of *Elephant Boy* was really the result of a mosaic of talents, most particularly of the Korda brothers, who shaped and reshaped the film, finally completing it in England. It has already been mentioned that Flaherty had little to show after many months of filming, although his touch was certainly evident in every scene containing long shadows, a result of his penchant for filming during early morning and late afternoon when the sun is low in the sky. Flaherty's work is also notable for its sparse dialogue; he devoutly believed that "a picture is worth a thousand words", an adage he consistently proved in his films.

Ultimately, though, *Elephant Boy* does not belong to either Flaherty or Korda, or even Kipling, but to Sabu, whose brilliance outshines the sub-tropical Indian sun. His impact upon audiences was immediate and enduring. Forever after he would be known as "The Elephant Boy", a sobriquet which grew tiresome in later years, but which helped to secure his placement among the top rank of motion picture stars. Few other child actors before or since have made such an initial impression. Lacking any kind of acting background, but with a smile as broad as the Ganges and the ability to charm the stripes off a tiger, Sabu shot to stardom in his very first vehicle. Moviegoers the world over flocked to see the first dark-skinned boy with a foreign accent to star in a major British production.

From his camaraderie with the awesome Kala Nag, his grief at his father's death, and his final triumph in being dubbed "Toomai of the Elephants", Sabu, his eyes glistening with tears of pride, dominates the film. Small wonder that Zoltan Korda enlarged Toomai's role for his newly found small wonder now known as Sabu. One has only to view the prologue of *Elephant Boy* to know that one is witnessing the debut of a refreshing new star. Sabu's exuberance is more than apparent as he speaks to the audience, beginning with "I salute you, *sahibs*! How do you do?" He then launches into a synopsis of the action which is to follow, closing with, "And here is the beginning of our story" as he bows.

Though he is by far the smallest being in the film, Sabu soon cuts everyone down to size. In the opening scene, for example, he takes the great elephant Kala Nag to task for stealing his sugar cane. "You big robber!" he cries, shaking his fist. "I'll teach you! Didn't I say leave it? Lift up your foot!" He strikes the huge extremity with a small club. "Am I not your master? Foot up!" He repeats the blow. Such fearlessness and confidence before a creature many times his size increases the boy's stature figuratively if not literally.

Few though they are, the other actors merely react to Sabu. He is the catalyst in this tale of elephants and men. Only Irawatha, eas-ily the largest being in the film, offers any real competition for the acting honors. His "mad scene" after being beaten with a length of chain by Rham Lahl, the evil *mahout*, is

Elephant Boy (London Films, 1937)
Sabu and Kala Nag

a tour de force. He breaks his bonds and races through the jungle, leveling a village in the process. Footage of Irawatha shot during his *musth* period was combined with shots of a real rogue elephant, resulting in a scene of sin-gular power. Viewed today, *Elephant Boy* is still enjoyable. Save for the presence of the British, there are no elements linking it to the past, so it has not dated.

Aside from the photography, the critic for *The London Times* felt that the best thing about the film was its star: "But as there has to be a story, it is a great thing that the Indian boy, Sabu, plays the chief part in it. He may be a

born actor, or he may have that natural and unselfconscious grace which can be recorded so well in a film, but whichever it is, he is exactly right for Mr. Flaherty's art and a perfect foil for his elephant." How observant that reviewer was! Time and time again Sabu would prove that he was both a born actor and possessed of "that natural and unselfconscious grace" which registers so rarely on film. Another favorable review was that of John Grierson (1898-1972), who had used the term "documen-

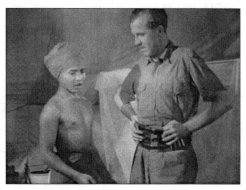

Elephant Boy (London Films, 1937)
Sabu and Walter Hudd

tary" for the first time in February 1926, when describing *Moana*, Flaherty's idyll of the South Seas. A noted documentary filmmaker himself, Grierson pointed to the truth with which Flaherty imbued his scenes as evidence of the film's quality.

Elephant Boy opened in New York on April 23, where it began its conquest of the American market, winning many more fans for the ever-smiling Indian lad. Among them was Frank S. Nugent, whose assessment of its star in *The New York Times* was most flattering: "Sabu...is a sunny-faced, manly little youngster, whose naturalness beneath the camera's scrutiny should bring blushes to the faces of the precocious wonder-children of Hollywood. He's a much better actor than the British players Mr. Flaherty tried to disguise behind frizzed beards and Indian names." About the film, he added: "Having a simple story at its heart, it has had the wisdom and good taste to tell it simply and without recourse to synthetic sensationalism."

Accompanying Sabu to the premiere in Paris were Robert Flaherty and the Borradailes. It was the boy's first time in an airplane and he was a bit nervous, having never before been in or on anything more than ten feet off the ground. He overcame his uneasiness with his characteristic courage and self-assurance, two traits he developed early and which remained with him throughout his all-too brief life.

After the premiere, a group of young French actors showed their admiration for their Indian colleague by giving him a reception. It is reported that Sabu showed remarkable poise, charming all present, even though he did not understand their language.

Elephant Boy took the prize for Best Direction as the official British entry at the 1937 Venice Film Festival, with Robert Flaherty and Zoltan Korda sharing the honors. This was icing on the cake for the debut film of the silver screen's newest and most unique child star.

Back in Britain the young Indian was given as much star treatment as he could handle. Having posed for a bronze bust by the renowned sculptor Lady Kennet in July of

1936, he now sat for a portrait in oils by the noted painter A. Egerton Cooper, which was reproduced in the May 4, 1938 issue of *The London Sketch*. Sabu also appeared on several radio programs broadcast from Alexandria Palace and once, with cameraman Osmond Borradaile, on the popular B.B.C. show *In Town Tonight*. The apex of all this attention occurred when Queen Mary toured Denham Studios and Sabu was introduced to her. It was there, too, that mail addressed to London Films' latest find began flowing in steadily, an indication of the rising popularity of Korda's latest star. The ex-journalist took notice and set about to find a fresh property with which to showcase the singular talents of this hot young personality from the Indian sub-continent.

Sabu was indeed fortunate in having Alexander Korda for a mentor. Together with his two brothers, the producer headed an exceedingly talented triumvirate. Alex, of course, was the business mind who could also turn out a sophisticated comedy film without much ado. Vincent had studied art at the College of Industrial Art in Budapest and afterwards with the famous painter Bela Grunwald. His set designs probably contributed more to the look of a Korda picture than any other element. His fractured English was also the cause of much mirth among his British colleagues over the years. Zoltan was the rebellious brother who loved filming in remote locales. Possessed of a deep feeling for indigenous peoples, he strove to show their dignity in the films he directed. It was natural that he should take to Sabu as he did, given the youngster's charm and intelligence.

Also to the youth's advantage was having the facilities of the most modern studio in Europe available to him. Denham Studios, which had opened in May of 1936, had been designed by the American architect Jack Okey, who had also blueprinted the studios used by First National and Paramount. Numbering among its many structures seven large soundstages and Denham Laboratories, the first Technicolor lab in Great Britain, Alex Korda's dream village also had its own water supply and the largest private electrical plant in the nation. Sprawled over a 165-acre site along the Colne River in Buckinghamshire, Denham embodied England's attempt to resist further inroads from Hollywood and shine entirely on its own.

After his initial spree in the limelight, it was back to Beaconstone for Sabu, where his honesty and enthusiasm won him many friends. He participated in sports and indulged his fascination with mechanical things, especially those capable of carrying him from one point to another at high speeds. Automobiles and planes

Elephant Boy (London Films, 1937) Sabu

were now his passions; he once lost a tennis match when he kept his eye on an airplane rather than on the ball. Life was good for him now, but he did not forget his roots, often writing to friends in India and keeping his door open for any visitors.

Progressing exceptionally well in his studies at school, Sabu waited patiently for the projects that were sure to come. The Kordas, he was certain, would not let him down.

Chapter Four

The Drum

In the months following the release of *Elephant Boy*, Alex Korda became anxious as he searched for a suitable follow-up project for his exciting new find. Never one to remain still for any length of time, the hyper Hungarian was not about to let Sabu rest on his laurels considering the investment he had in the youngster. A film idea designed to highlight the boy's uniqueness was needed, and needed fast. If London Films was going to continue the pace set with *The Private Life of Henry VIII*, Korda had to keep his company of top-notch technicians at Denham busy applying their well-honed skills to several projects at once. Production was the name of the game; idle soundstages meant angry investors (in this case, the Prudential Assurance Company). So a constant stream of exceptional properties was imperative in order to prevent unhappiness both among the money men and the theater owners.

One project considered as a vehicle for Sabu was *Bur-*

mese Silver, to be directed by Michael Powell (1905-1990), a young genius who had recently been signed by Korda Productions. The political situation in Southeast Asia had become so volatile, however, what with the recent Japanese invasion of the Chinese mainland, that sending a film crew to nearby Burma would have proven too risky. So the idea, based on a World War I novel by J. Storer Clouston about German spies at Scapa Flow, was scrapped.

Korda's most pressing quest came to an end when A.E.W. Mason handed him a treatment tailored for Sabu's special talents. Mason (1865-1948), a popular novelist for over four decades, was the creator of many works which evoked the glories of the British Empire. In such stirring books as *The Four Feathers* (1902) and *The Broken Road* (1907) set in the Sudan and India, respectively, he showed the courage and stamina of the British soldier as he fought for queen and country in two of the more remote corners of that empire.

After London Films' *Fire Over England*, a less than adequate adaptation of another of Mason's novels, was released in late 1936, the author was given *carte blanche* by Korda in writing a new scenario featuring a major part for Sabu. The only stipulation was that a drum had to figure prominently in the plot. Alex apparently felt that Sabu and a drum were like spaghetti and meatballs, or goulash and slivovitz; all right by themselves, but ever so much better together. This proved to be no problem for Mason. From his research he was familiar with Sir Mortimer Durand's *The Making of a Frontier*, which chronicled the Second Afghan War (1878-1880). Contained therein is the legend of the Yudeni Drum, an instrument with alleged magical powers. Using this as the basis for "the Sacred Drum of Tokot", the experienced author fashioned a film outline in very short order. (A revised version of Mason's exciting tale appeared in the November 1937 issue of *The Strand* magazine and the story was later issued as "a book of the film" after the picture's release.)

With a working title of *Mutiny in the Mountains*, a special unit from London Films was sent to the Khyber Pass in northern India, where cameraman Osmond Borra-daile photographed footage for establishing shots. Zoltan Korda arranged the loan of three thousand members of the Mehtar of Chitral's personal bodyguard for an added touch of realism. However, if he thought that their presence would facilitate matters, he had another think coming. When a certain number of these troops were required to be "killed" on film, those chosen refused to fall down. The reason: they feared that if they "died" in the picture, their movie careers would end then and there. After much explaining and gesticulating on the part of no fewer than six interpreters, the matter was settled, and the selected men obediently "died".

All the heavy equipment of a film crew was carried through the Khyber Pass by hardy pack mules as the humans struggled through the rarefied air of some of the world's tallest peaks. At heights as great as 11,000 feet, actors and cameramen plied their trades while porters raced up the mountains gathering quantities of lightly packed snow to place around the metal-lined trunks which held the tins of film. Despite all the danger involved, not a single accident occurred. As an economy move the regular cast and crew stayed much closer to home, filming in the rocky hills of Cwm Bychen in North Wales. This location was chosen after veterans of the Afghan campaigns were consulted as to which areas in the British Isles most closely resembled the rough terrain of the Afghan frontier. Director Zoltan Korda's use of this rugged area of Wales is masterly, although it was utilized only in the march of Carruthers' detachment toward Tokot and his initial meeting with Prince Azim. With John Greenwood's driving music accenting the action, the soldiers are shown from several angles as they forge relentlessly onward up and down the steep mountain trails. Korda also put the Indian footage to good use at the beginning and end of the film, nicely framing his picture with sweeping vistas of wild mountain landscapes.

Although Lajos Biro had adapted Mason's outline, with the screenplay written by Arthur Wimperis, Patrick Kirwin, and Hugh Grey, Mason was still present every day at Denham, where the interiors were filmed. He wished to make sure that the resulting film would not be the disappointment

Fire Over England had been. Two army officers were hired as technical advisors as well, to insure full accuracy for the film's military details.

The Drum (London Films, 1938) U.S. Poster

Sabu, as Prince Azim, was given excellent support in his second film, now called *The Drum*, his first in Technicolor. Welshman Roger Livesey (1906-1976) portrayed Capt. Carruthers, head of the British residency, with his usual charm and wit. As his wife, twenty-year-old Valerie Hobson (1917-1998) made a lovely English rose. Miss Hobson recalled those long-ago days in a letter to the author: "I enjoyed making the picture very much...we were all colour-conscious as to make-up and clothes, with many tests. The atmosphere on the set was relaxed and warm - most of the actors knew each other (as was mostly the case in early film days in England - the artists being recruited from the stage). Sabu was very alert and had much charm. He was eager to do well and was 'co-operative' with everyone. He had an aunt (?) on the set to whom he returned after each rehearsal, or take. She was a quiet, very pretty Indian lady, to whom I often spoke although she was rather shy." This lady was probably the tutor hired by Alex Korda, as Sabu had no living relatives save for his brother Dastagir. Portly Francis L. Sullivan (1903-1956), who later became noted for his Dickensian roles in two of David Lean's productions, played the governor. The part of the bloodthirsty, anti-British Prince Ghul went to Canadian actor Raymond Massey (1896-1983), he of the blazing eyes and curling lip. Possessed of one of the most resonant voices in film, the future portrayer of Abraham Lincoln made the most of his screen time, in this, his final performance for London Films. Playing Bill Holder, the drummer boy chum of Prince Azim, was young Desmond Tester (1919-2002), who had considerable acting experience, having been on the West End stage since 1931 at the age of twelve. He had already appeared in several films, including Alfred Hitchcock's *Sabotage* in 1936 and was the top male child actor in British films at the time. Tester remains unique among all Sabu's fellow actors as the sole male close to Sabu's age with whom the Indian teen could interact.

During production, the two got along famously. Their scenes together reflect their liking for each other, lending a touch of realism to their on-screen relationship. In a letter to this writer dated November 1993, Mr. Tester recalled: "I had seen and admired Sabu in *Elephant Boy* and was pleased to be cast in *The Drum*. He was easy to work with and a very good actor I thought. ... I had been in the business for several years. I believed I could recognize an actor. I do not remember how old Sabu was, but certainly several years younger than I. As you know, anything more than a year at that age makes all the difference. I liked Sabu but only saw him while working."

Mr. Tester also told a tale from school in his letter: "I wonder did Sabu witness that lovely row between Raymond Massey and Zoltan Korda? Korda wanted Massey to play some scene in a way which Massey did not, as usual, quite agree with; saying something like 'No, Zolie, I feel that as the Khan I should...etc.' To which Korda said, 'You are my dog, I am not your dog. You do vot I tell you.' A long tea break for the cooling off."

Tester later appeared on early British television, writing his own one-man acts for children's programs aired over the British Broadcasting Corporation's channel. Receiving an offer to act in a comedy opening in Melbourne, Australia, in 1956, he emigrated "Down Under" where he later had his own television show. Originating in Sydney, it was made for children and titled "Channel Ninepins". Tester additionally appeared in 125 episodes of *The Kaper Cops*. He also recalled in his letter: "Whenever *The Drum* was shown [on television] I got notes from the kids about...what was Sabu like...?" Desmond married while in Australia and sired five children. After his show's ten-year run ended, he acted in films up until 1984. He spent his retirement years enjoying the natural wonders of Australia until his death in late 2002.

As in his first picture, Sabu had a close call during filming. In a shot calling for him to ride his lively white Arabian stallion along a precipitous mountain trail, he almost collided with the leader

The Drum (London Films, 1938) Sabu

of a group of Indian lancers approaching from the opposite direction. He pulled up, but one of his horse's hind legs slipped over the edge of the trail. One of the lancers quickly grabbed the boy about the waist and pulled him from his mount. His action also allowed the animal to regain its footing and avoid serious injury.

Sabu acquitted himself well in his role as the prince, giving orders with real authority, maintaining a regal bearing, and riding a horse like a veteran cavalryman, all the while exuding enough charm to retake India from the British single-handedly. Although he would forever be associated with elephants, his uncanny affinity with all animals became evident in this film, and even more in future roles.

After five weeks on location, the unit returned to Denham for interiors. There, Vincent Korda (1896-1979) displayed his great talent by designing exceedingly realistic bazaars, palaces, barracks, and exotic buildings. Filmed in vivid Technicolor, his sets literally draw the viewer into the exotic hill country of far-off India. *The Drum* contains all the multi-faceted trademarks of a typical Korda production as well. Humor is present in the persons of a sergeant of a Scottish company and the private he delights in persecuting. When explaining the differences in the local customs, the sergeant quickly turns to the private and asks, "Have ya got that, Kelly?" or "Ya hear that, Kelly?" Pvt. Kelly gives the non-com his come-uppance just before the troops leave for a feast at the palace of the khan of Tokot. The sergeant is instructing his men how to behave "in the home of a Mohammedan prince": "Whether it's snakes or stomach wagglin', I want to see a look of rapture on your faces. Know what a look of rapture is, Kelly?" he sneers. "Like what gunner Wilson 'ad when 'e strained 'isself with the 'owitzer!" replies Kelly with a straight face. There is also a bit of unintentional humor. Knowing that he is very likely entering a trap by attending the Khan's banquet, Carruthers wisely leaves part of his command at the barracks, with orders to proceed on the double to the palace when a certain signal is given. As he leaves for the palace, the officer in charge of those troops exhorts him to "Have a good time, sir!"

The first-rate photography in *The Drum* is the work of Georges Perinal (1897-1965) on the interiors and Denham exteriors and of Osmond Borradaile on the Indian second-unit exteriors. Their styles mesh perfectly, presenting fascinating views of craggy mountain passes and the ornate splendor and even squalor of eastern architecture. As usual in a London Films' picture, production values are high. Alex Korda never spared expense to make his pictures shine on screen, and every penny shows. No critic ever said a Korda film looked cheap. The attention to even the smallest detail in *The Drum* is such as to require repeated viewings to absorb it all. The producer's formula was simple: hire the best technicians in every field in order to obtain the best results.

Zoltan Korda's respect for indigenous peoples and disdain of imperialism is evident by the fact he pokes mild fun at the British, but not the Indians. He gives the racism of the time exposure by showing the term "beggar" being used by the British in referring to the natives. He also illustrates the stuffiness of the British officials by allowing the Indian characters, particularly Prince Ghul, to be much more fascinating individuals. Both the British and the Indians are bound by rigid sets of rules and traditions. Ghul has already stated his desire to recreate the past in fervent words to his secret followers: "I see a wave; a wave of men. Lean, hard, hungry free men from the hills, swooping down on the fat, soft, comfortable slaves of the plains, their white throats ripe for the knife. It is a story as old as time. I see a river, the river Jhelum. The Jhelum, where the old Mogul Empire thrived. I see the mosques and domes rise again; the palaces of Shah Jahan."

Mohammed Khan, the native leader loyal to the British, is on to him and warns Capt. Carruthers: "Ghul is a madman who dreams high dreams," a statement the Briton is only too willing to believe. His suspicions are borne out later when Ghul invites the British to a banquet on the final night of a holy feast. This proves to be a trap for the foreigners, as Ghul has positioned machine guns at strategic points in the palace with the gunners awaiting a signal on the Sacred Drum. Fortunately for the British, Azim learns of the plot and arrives in time to beat his own signal, taught him by Holder, on the Sacred Drum, alerting Carruthers to the danger and averting annihilation of the foreign troops.

Ghul, like all dedicated madmen, is not interested solely in power. He fully appreciates feminine beauty, as when introduced to Mrs. Carruthers he proclaims, "In our country we have many orchards with beautiful and delicate blossoms, but the most lovely of all is now in the British residence." Massey's rendering of his lines imbues them with the passion they deserve; his is one of the three characters which breathe real life into the proceedings. Prince Azim's, of course, is another, and the third is Bill Holder, the drummer boy who befriends the prince. As interpreted by Desmond Tester, Holder is a no-nonsense fellow who will boldly assert his rights when he catches Azim playing his drum, yet quakes in his kilt when caught smoking by the sergeant. While being beaten for this transgression, however, he makes no sound. Holder is also intensely loyal to his young Indian friend, and is ready to help him whenever the need arises.

While Zoltan Korda may have preferred the cultures of distant lands, he retains his objectivity with his scenes of the men of the Scottish company seated around a fire at night singing "Loch Lomond", and continues with the same group showing off their "sword dance" to the Indians during the banquet. He further balances the cultural scale by including considerable footage of that other symbol of British imperialism, the bagpipes (ironically, an instrument invented in Asia). Besides the conventional use of them in marching columns, Korda includes a parade of pipers at a traditional officers' dinner. Despite this nod to imperialist pageantry, one cannot help but feel that the sun is setting on the British Empire. In fact, it is little short of incredible that it took a trio of Jewish Hungarian expatriates to best define the dying days of England's glory.

The final product stands among the best adventure films ever made. With its rousing battle scenes and colorful tableaux of the mysterious East, *The Drum* fits snugly between Zoltan Korda's other epics of empire, *Sanders of the River* (1935) and *The Four Feathers* (1939). It also holds up very well against its competition from Hollywood that year. In fact, the only U.S. release in the adventure film genre that can be considered superior is the classic *The Adventures of Robin Hood*. Even here it is difficult to compare the near fantasy of the Warner Bros. production with the gritty realism of *The Drum*.

Most importantly, *The Drum* proved that young Sabu was perfectly capable of carrying a film on his own small but strong back. After the film's release in England on April 9, 1938, almost a year to the day after that of *Elephant Boy*, his popularity soared so high that his fan mail increased to over 100 letters a day. No child star of British films up until that time had inspired such a following. This was the spur that Alex Korda needed to begin planning a major career for the boy. It was during this time that RKO, an American studio, approached Korda in an effort to borrow Sabu for the challenging title role in their own pro-empire picture, *Gunga Din*, which began shooting in July of 1938. They felt the youngster was a natural for the title role of Kipling's immortal water-bearer, but Korda was already thinking ahead to *The Thief of Bagdad* and could not be persuaded to lend the lad for any amount. The part eventually fell to veteran character actor Sam Jaffe (1891-1984), and the film that followed, though magnificent in most respects, suffered a bit by being in black and white. Aware of the appropriateness of the personality whom he was replacing, Jaffe later admitted that in order to give the best performance possible, he modeled himself after Sabu. That is some praise for a relative newcomer, especially such a young one, to receive from an established colleague.

As a reward for his fine work in *The Drum*, Korda sent

Sabu on his first trip to the United States to promote the film and appear at its premiere in New York City. Aboard the *Aquitania*, the youthful star must have been both thrilled and curious as to what new wonders awaited him in the greatest city in the western world. Upon disembarking, he assumed the role of tourist, though not just any tourist. He and his two bearded Sikh bodyguards caused more than a stir among Americans unused to seeing such foreign apparitions in those pre-war Depression days. With their dark skins and brightly-colored turbans, they were living proof that there was indeed a world of mystery as described by Kipling and Mason beyond the oceans bounding America. Sabu was duly feted by press and public, giving endless interviews and accepting honors from various youth organizations during his stay.

The film, the title of which had been pluralized to *Drums* in the U.S., probably because it sounded louder and more action-oriented, opened at New York's premiere movie palace, Radio City Music Hall, on September 30. Sabu again made a personal appearance and was warmly received. Reviews were generally excellent, citing specifically the film's color photography and action. Critic B.P. Crisler of *The New York Times* found other elements to praise as well: "Mr. Korda, or somebody, has endowed his production with a number of solid cinematic virtues, including a richly authentic colonial atmosphere..." "Lean back and enjoy...be charmed by the rightful prince, Sabu,

and chuckle pater-
nally at that scamp
of a drummer boy."
The few negative
comments were
aimed at its imperi-
alist elements which
actually caused riot-
ing in some Indian
cities, where it was
felt Sabu's role as
the British-support-
ing Prince Azim was
a betrayal of India's
growing indepen-
dence movement.

Carole Lombard takes Sabu for a ride

There the film was either cut drastically or pulled from cir-
culation. Despite that hostile reception, it became an international box-office hit and garnered The City of Venice
Cup at the 1938 Venice Film Festival. Sabu's U.S. itinerary
also included Washington, D.C., where he was welcomed
by President Roosevelt and his wife, Eleanor. Mrs. Roosevelt greatly impressed the young Indian with her own
knowledge of elephants, indeed an odd choice of animals for a life-long Democrat. The adolescent actor also
visited Hollywood, where he toured the set of *Made for
Each Other* (1939), which starred Carole Lombard, one of

Sabu's favorite actresses. She won his undying love when she took him around the studio aboard her motor scooter.

The French premiere of the picture found Sabu, Desmond Tester, the Korda brothers and their wives, and the Borradailes, flying over the English Channel to Paris. There the two youngsters appeared on stage in their costumes from the film. Later, Tester did the town with members of the press, while fourteen-year-old Sabu had to return to his hotel room, a victim of age discrimination.

It was not long afterwards that Alex Korda lost control of Denham Studios. For over a year the studio had been suffering losses, and the large sums that had been advanced to it had not been repaid due to Korda's personal and cinematic extravagances, which the grosses could not cover. By New Year's Day 1939, a deal which amalgamated Korda's Denham Studio with J. Arthur Rank's Pinewood Studio was made by the Prudential Assurance Company. Upsetting as this was, it did not deter the ambitious producer from his next project. He had purchased the rights to Douglas Fairbanks' *The Thief of Bagdad* (1924) through his partnership in United Artists, the company which released his productions in America. He also remained a part-owner of Technicolor, Inc., and retained his interests in United Artists and Denham Laboratories. So the imaginative and cultured émigré, unmoved and unbowed, became a tenant producer at his former studio and began putting together what was to become his greatest achievement.

Chapter Five

The Thief of Bagdad

The year 1939 was to be a memorable one for Alex Korda and for the world. In March, the erstwhile head of London Films formed a new company, Alexander Korda Productions. That same month he began work on his most ambitious project to date, a remake of the classic Douglas Fairbanks fantasy *The Thief of Bagdad*, an extraordinary motion picture which had captivated audiences everywhere fifteen years earlier. In June he married his foremost leading lady, the stunningly beautiful Merle Oberon. In September, both Great Britain and France declared war on Nazi Germany, effectively commencing the conflict which became known as World War II. And that fateful month found *The Thief of Bagdad* still in production.

The story goes that at a banquet following the Hollywood premiere of *Drums*, Alex was sitting across from Douglas Fairbanks when Sabu entered the room. Spotting him, the producer asked Fairbanks if he could buy the rights to *The Thief of Bagdad* for his dynamic young star. The swashbuckling actor took one look at the handsome youth and said, "It's a deal. The rights are yours."

The Thief of Bagdad (London Films/ UA, 1940) Conrad Veidt as Jaffar

When he had purchased the rights to this epic fantasy, Korda had seen the project as a perfect vehicle not only for Sabu, but for the other big foreign name on his payroll, the great German actor Conrad Veidt (1893-1943).

Veidt had left his native country after the rise of Nazism and come to Britain, where he signed with Gaumont-British, appearing in six films for them between 1933 and 1936. When that company hit financial hard times, Veidt was advised by a friend to contact Alex Korda, which he did. He soon became one of the famed producer's top stars.

Around these exceptional performers Alex began assembling as cosmopolitan a collection of technical experts as could possibly be found. As a start, Ludwig Berger (1892-1969), a countryman of Veidt's, was signed to an airtight contract, giving him complete control over the new film in the capacity of director. Berger, a Ph.D. in art history whose real name was Ludwig Bamberger, had collaborated with the celebrated Max Reinhardt on many Shake-spearean productions at the renowned Deutsches Theatre in Berlin. He later directed several films in his homeland before journeying to the U.S. in 1927. Returning to Europe in 1932, he helmed films in Germany, Holland and France before being summoned to Denham by Alex Korda. Brother Vincent, representing Hungary, headed the art department crew, which consisted of Britons Johnny Mills, Percy (Pop) Day, and Peter Ellenshaw, as well as American William Cameron Menzies (1896-1957), who had cut his designing teeth on the 1924 United Artists version of the story. Menzies actually designed the entire production and directed all the miniature work, although, along with Zoltan Korda, who created the sets, their positions as associated producers were not credited onscreen. He had also been the production designer for *Gone with the Wind* (1939) and other notable productions. Georges Perinal, an expert on lighting, was given the task of photographing the monumental work. After carving out a solid career in his native France beginning as a projectionist for Pathé in 1913 and continuing on to photograph the early 1930s films of René Clair, he succumbed to the Korda charm and began working for London Films in 1933. Having proven his ability with color on *The Drum* and *The Four Feathers*, Perinal was the obvious choice to lens *The Thief of Bagdad*. Osmond Borradaile, the Canadian who had contributed so strikingly to the look of Sabu's first two films as well as being the boy's discoverer, was chosen to handle the foreign location photography. The screenplay was to be a collaboration between a Briton and a Hungarian. Veteran stage and screen character actor Miles Malleson, who was also a writer, would adapt Lajos Biro's screenplay and write the dialogue. Malleson, noted for his translations of the great 17th-century French comic playwright Moliére, also landed the coveted role of the foolish old sultan, father of the Princess and collector of mechanical toys.

Biro used elements from several of *The Arabian Nights* tales in his screenplay, including the mechanical flying horse from "The Story of the Magic Horse", the genie in the bottle from "The Story of the Fisherman and the Brass Bottle", the magic carpet from "The Story of Prince Ahmed and the Fairy Perie Banou", and the magical transformation of the Thief into a dog from "The Story of Sidi Nouman", along with some original incidents. Writing the score for this Technicolor fantasy would be another Korda countryman, Budapest-born Miklos Rozsa (1907-1995). The thirty-two-year-old composer had earned a fine reputation on the Continent as a creator of first-rate orchestral works prior to his joining London Films. It was at the instigation of French director Jacques Feyder that Rozsa was given the opportunity to compose film music. Feyder was an admirer of his and decided that Miklos should be the one to write the score for the film he was currently directing. Feyder convinced Alex Korda to sign him, and

Knight Without Armour (1937) became the first of scores of memorable scores to flow from Rozsa's talented pen. For *The Thief of Bagdad*, though, Rozsa had to play a waiting game while Alex figured out how to get Ludwig Berger to drop *his* choice for composer. Berger had selected Oscar Straus, a Viennese composer best known for his 1909 operetta *The Chocolate Soldier*, which had been purchased by MGM as a vehicle for Nelson Eddy. Straus' projected music for *The Thief of Bagdad* proved totally unsuitable for the mood of the picture, as Muir Matheson, London Films' musical director, quickly pointed out to Korda. The producer was now in a real dilemma, for he had given Berger complete artistic control. His backers would not supply the necessary monies unless Berger directed, and Berger would not direct unless Straus composed the score. Alex pondered the situation for a few weeks. Finally, he told Rozsa to write some songs and play them loudly from the office next to Berger's whenever the director was present. After several days, Berger became curious and asked the composer what he was doing. The latter told him that he had his own ideas for the film's score and played the songs once more for him. Berger was won over completely. Miklos was in and Oscar was out, and the end result was one of the finest films scores ever written.

Also in was Sir Robert Vansittart (1881-1957), permanent Under-Secretary of the British Foreign Service. His familiarity with the Persian language impressed Alex Korda to the extent that the diplomat was allowed to try his hand at writing lyrics for Rozsa's songs. Vansittart spent all his spare time during that last uneasy pre-war summer working on the mid-Eastern fantasy. The charming simplicity of the words he labored over definitely add to the enchantment of the film. Preferring anonymity, Vansittart was listed in the credits as Robert Denham, taking the name of the studio as his alias.

Los Angeles-born William Hornbeck (1901-1983) was to manage the editing. A former head of the editing department at the legendary Mack Sennett Studios, he honed his craft at London Films from 1934 through 1942. He went on to win six Oscars in post-war Hollywood.

The cast selection proved to be most felicitous, once all the assignments had been set. Sabu was, of course, the inspiration for this ambitious undertaking, so Biro tailored his screenplay to fit him as the title character. Veidt was a fine choice for the villain of the piece, with his famous haunting "demonic" look and wide-ranging acting ability. Vivien Leigh, Korda's leading actress at the time, was originally set to play the Princess, but *Gone with the Wind* intervened. So Korda picked twenty-one-year-old June Duprez, who was so impressive as the female lead in *The Four Feathers*, for the part. The daughter of American vaudevillian Fred Duprez, the exotic beauty and innocence of the London-born-and-raised actress proved ideal for the role. For Ahmad, the young king, Korda had wanted

Jon Hall, an American actor who had been the male lead in John Ford's *The Hurricane* (1937) and who was destined to star in three films with Sabu. Unable to obtain Hall's services, Alex chose a young actor named John Justin, whose agent had urged him to test for the role. Justin had studied briefly at the Royal Academy of Dramatic art and was currently appearing in a West End play. Asked by Brian McFarlane in a 1990 interview how he had started with such a "plum part", Mr. Justin replied that he had a very good agent who urged him to visit Denham for a test.

"I was sick of auditions and was about to give the whole thing up, so I went out to Denham, quite relaxed for a change. I went onto the huge stage which had a boat in the middle of it in which was a little Indian boy. I put on some kind of costume and got into the boat with the little boy, Sabu; he was very funny and clever and utterly unafraid of all the film people, and this helped me. The two of us sent the whole test up. Naturally I would have worked much harder at it, but I did it quite casually, and left assuming I had missed out. Two days later the front page of one of the newspapers had me on it, with headlines! This whole publicity campaign had started, and I had been cast without even knowing about it." (McFarlane's fascinating interview with Mr. Justin can be read in its entirety in his *An Autobiography of the British Cinema*, Methuen, London, England, 1997.)

John, who had been born to an Argentinean father and an English mother in London in November 1917, ultimately gave a rather vapid portrayal of King Ahmed, one far removed from Jon Hall's vigorous heroics at the time. But it was in keeping with the role of a naive love struck king, and left the action mostly for Sabu.

The Thief of Bagdad (London Films/UA, 1940) Rex Ingram as the genie

African-American actor Rex Ingram, who was so effective as "De Lawd" in Warner Bros.' all-black musical *The Green Pastures* (1936), was recruited to portray another awesome being, this time the gigantic genie who is tricked into granting Abu three wishes.

Despite this talented roster of technicians and actors, things managed to go amiss. When Alex Korda returned from his honeymoon in July, he immediately found fault with everything. Disappointed with the work of Biro and Malleson, he had them rewrite the script almost daily. He was likewise displeased with Vincent's initial conception of Bagdad, and told his younger sibling in no uncertain terms to build bigger and brighter sets. The producer then realized he had erred in hiring Berger to direct. It seems that the good doctor had it in mind to make the film entirely within the studio in the German fashion of the

1920s. Alex had envisioned a picture with much broader scope, even incorporating scenes shot at various locations in North Africa. Unable to fire Berger due to the terms of the contract, the canny Korda began a campaign of psychological sabotage designed to force the director to submit. He first brought in Michael Powell to view Berger's test footage. The thirty-three-year-old Powell had apprenticed under the great Irish silent film director Rex Ingram in the mid-twenties before a stint with an up-and-coming young British director named Alfred Hitchcock. He next spent several years directing "quota quickies", the infamous result of Hollywood's saturation of the British film market. Made on shoestring budgets, these films were designed to insure at least a certain percentage of films in British theaters were actually British. They provided a valuable training ground for many actors and directors who later achieved prominence in the industry.

Powell then came to Korda's attention with a highly original production filmed in the Shetland Islands called *The Edge of the World* (1937). Korda hired Powell for *Thief*, along with Tim Whelan (1893-1957), an American who had written material for comic actor Harold Lloyd before becoming a director in Britain. The former was given the large-scale scenes and most of those with Sabu and Veidt, while the latter handled the humorous action scenes. That left Berger to direct the intimate scenes with the romantic leads.

While Berger was thus engaged, Powell was off to Cornwall with Sabu and Osmond Borradaile to start shooting Alex's conception of the film. It was the first meeting between the Canterbury-born director and the former stable boy from India. In the first volume of his autobiography, *A Life in Movies*, Powell wrote that he found Sabu "enchanting," adding that "He never had the slightest bit of star fever about him. He said: 'I and my family are eating well and sleeping well and that's all that matters to me." The two became life-long friends. Finding the selected site too confining for their purposes, Powell took his unit to the rugged coast of Pembrokeshire in South Wales. There the scene when Abu's boat is washed ashore and he discovers the bottle containing the genie was filmed on a picturesque stretch of beach.

Back at Denham, Powell and Whelan were getting the production into high gear. Handling every twist and turn in the story with the determination born of belief in the film's potential, the inspired pair worked like dervishes to make the picture worthy of its source material, the age-old tales from *The Arabian Nights*. Powell also discussed ideas with Vincent Korda in an effort to make the color work for him, rather than his working for the color. It was the director who conceived the idea of painting a huge eye on the prow of Jaffar's ship, recalling an ancient practice of Arab sailors. This touch added to the eye motif which included Jaffar's evilly glittering orbs and the fabulous gem that served as the "eye" of the Goddess of Light. It was at Denham, too, that all of Conrad Veidt's scenes were shot.

Veidt was one of the most popular and prolific actors to emerge from the fertile studios of Berlin during the golden era of the German cinema in the 1920s. He had appeared in some ninety films in his homeland, and had brought much prior stage experience with him as well. Powell had been eager to work with the veteran star ever since he found himself at the same studio as Veidt. Although he had already directed him in a pair of espionage pictures, *The Spy in Black* (1939) and *Contraband* (1940), for two other companies, he now had Technicolor and could do wonders with Conrad's hypnotic blue eyes! In a conversation with this writer in 1986, Michael Powell recalled Conrad Veidt as "the finest actor I ever directed" and "the most charming and sophisticated heterosexual I ever met." Veidt's untimely death from a heart attack at the age of fifty in 1943 was a great loss to his profession as well as to his many fans. (On April 3, 1998, Veidt's ashes, along with those of his wife, Lily, were returned to London through the efforts of the Conrad Veidt Society, the international fan club devoted to him. They were placed in a mortuary which also contains the ashes of Sir Alexander Korda. Until Lily's death in 1980, they had been kept in Ferncliff Cemetery in New York state. Her ashes were mixed with his and held by a nephew in Los Angeles until 1993, when he presented them to James Rathlesberger, the head of the Society.)

So throughout the spring and summer of 1939 Michael Powell and Tim Whelan worked their magic on Denham's vast soundstages, back lots and surrounding area, happily putting the cast of thousands through its paces. John Aldred, who went to work for Korda's London Films at the new Denham studio in 1938, later offered some personal recollections. He reports that the large *The Thief of Bagdad* sets were built on the "City Square" lot, so called because Everytown City had been constructed there for the science-fiction film *Things to Come* in 1936. That proved to be a box-office disaster due to its unnatural dialogue and H. G. Wells, who had been hired to direct, being unfamiliar with filmmaking. The picture is best remembered for Vincent Korda's huge sets, including Everytown (which in the film reverts to barbarism) and its accurate prediction of World War II. Just three years later it served as the magical port of Basra with a large Arab sailing ship on wheels (the harbor itself was quite shallow) pulled into the harbor by a tractor. Vincent, he says, had used this idea before during *Sanders of the River.*

Meanwhile, behind the scenes, Korda's special effects experts had to tackle the logistics of making the various mythical beings and objects look convincing in the then-difficult Technicolor process. Among those are a mechanical flying horse, a flying carpet, and a flying genie of Brobdignagian proportions. The crew began with the biggest problem, that of the genie with the jet-black hair.

The genie's hand, foot, and part of his head and shoulder had to be shown in close-up, so giant models of each were made in clay. Plaster casts were used to make the 36 sections needed for the shape of the hand;

The Thief of Bagdad (London Films/UA, 1940) Sabu tries out the genie's hand for size

papier-mâché parts were made from those. Since the fingers and thumb had to move, machinery was placed inside them. A very life-like rubber solution was used for the skin; the thickness served to conceal the joints in the papier-mâché parts. The foot was done in the same fashion, save for the interior mechanism, since, thankfully, the genie did not have to wiggle his toes. Matching the "skin" on these models to the color of Ingram's flesh was the final step. This was accomplished simply by coating the parts with paint in the required tone.

The crew's next project was the mechanical flying horse. A life-size model was made from a real horse in papier-mâché in six sections. These pieces were slotted and locked together and covered with horse hide. Fans who look closely at the scene where the sultan mounts the horse will note that its right rear hoof breaks into several pieces. Surely this was noted during or after filming, but it was never corrected. For its flying scenes, as for all the flying scenes in the film, the traveling matte process was employed. Only the sequence of Sabu on the magic carpet required additional cinematic chicanery. When he flies over the marketplace of Bagdad, a hanging miniature of the city in the background was utilized.

Makeup for some of the principals likewise presented problems. To give the Princess the proper Eastern look, it was decided to pluck out the hairs of June Duprez's widow's peak rather than build up her forehead, which would have spoiled the contour of her exquisite face. Rex Ingram's character, on the other hand, was to be bald except for a scalp lock. A flesh-like synthetic rubber material, colored to match the tone of the actor's face, was used to make a cap. With the scalp lock in place, it was fitted over his head. Since the cap had to cover his ears as well, casts were made of those extremities and modified into the shape common to genies of that region. Mary Morris, who played Halima, servant to Veidt's evil vizier, also played the Silver Maid. For this, Jaffar's most diabolical creation, the makeup department spent weeks attempting to create the proper shade of blue greasepaint. They finally succeeded by mixing several together, devising a new color. Miss Morris had to spend four hours in makeup each day while the greasepaint was patted over her entire person and powder dusted over it to soften the effect. Ex-

tra makeup was ap-
plied to her face, es-
pecially on her eyes.
Her long, curved
nails were made
of cellulose with
bands at the base of
each which slipped
over her fingers.

The Thief of Bagdad (London Films/UA, 1940) Mary Morris, Conrad Veidt (back to camera)

Although Conrad Veidt's features needed no additional touches to make his Jaffar appear more sinister, gold dust was sprinkled over the highlights of his face to increase the sense of mystery and unworldliness.

Added to all those carefully prepared details were the superbly executed background paintings of Percy Day and the accompanying artwork used for the glass shots. Coupled with Vincent Korda's outstanding sets, Bagdad appeared on the screen as a vast city of immense walls, towering minarets, expansive bazaars and bustling water-fronts filled with multi-hued ethnic groups in flowing cos-tumes. Among these latter can be spotted some of the same Indian faces seen among the hunters in *Elephant Boy*. The Temple of the Dawn, which rests on the Roof of the World, and wherein resides the Goddess of Light and her blue-skinned aboriginal guardians, is an incred-ibly detailed miniature. Obviously inspired by illustrations of multi-limbed Hindu deities, Vincent Korda took a page from brother Alex's book (the theme of which is "More is more") and created a truly impressive idol which, even with hundreds of arms, appeared magnificently serene.

The technical effort put into *The Thief of Bagdad* set records for the time. Over 140 trick shots were used, and the scenes set in the palace of the Sultan of Basra were the most powerfully lit sequences in film up to that period. No indoor set of that size had ever before been constructed, not to mention being filmed in color, and it took high intensity arc lights to accomplish the feat. Much of the credit must go to British optical effects cameraman Tom Howard. This was a real achievement in 1940, when the Technicolor process made it necessary to move three strips of film through the camera simultaneously. Great care also had to be taken to control the contrast of the film strips at every stage of filming, so that the color quality of the final scene would not deteriorate. For this purpose, an optical printer was specially adapted for Technicolor work and made accurate within 1/10,000 of an inch. The resulting brilliant color and painstaking effort were worth every cent spent; it literally dazzles the eye. From the tangerine-colored sails of Jaffar's ship to the peacock-blue buildings of Bagdad and the golden tents in the Land of Legend, the color fairly leaps off the screen.

The original 1924 *The Thief of Bagdad* had derived its success from both the powerful personality of its star, the irrepressible Douglas Fairbanks, and the awesome sets designed by William Cameron Menzies. It had been one of the glories of Hollywood in the silent era, and was a triumph of the fantasy genre. Its plot revolved around the adventures encountered by a lowly thief who disguises himself as a prince to win the hand of the caliph's daughter. Competing against three other suitors, a Persian, a Mongol and an Indian, the thief survives a number of exciting escapades before acquiring a magic chest. Returning to Bagdad, he finds the Mongol prince has had his army secretly infiltrate the city and it is now under his control. He also has had the Princess poisoned so that he would be the one to save her with the treasure he has discovered. Outside the gates, the thief creates an army by sprinkling magic powder from the chest on the ground and retakes Bagdad, winning the Princess in the process. Together they sail away on a flying carpet, presumably to Beverly Hills and happiness forever.

Biro's conception of the tale differs in many respects from the Fairbanks' version, the chief difference being the division of the lead role into two-characters - an adolescent thief and a young king. It is the king, of course, who is in love with a princess; but being of royal blood and therefore isolated, he is seriously lacking in street smarts. Providing the latter is the thief, who is also the more physical of the pair. Together they travel about a magical world, braving all kinds of thrilling adventures as they endeavor to keep the Princess from the clutches of the evil vizier,

Jaffar, who has usurped the throne, and restore the king to his rightful position. At one point, Jaffar's black magic renders the king and the thief powerless, the former being made blind and the latter transformed into a dog. It is in these circumstances that the pair is first seen, with Ahmad begging for alms on a Bagdad causeway. Shortly afterwards Ahmad recounts his previous life in a flashback sequence, and then the action returns to the present.

It can be said that Ahmad, the king, is the heart of the original character, and Abu, the thief, is the body and brain. The erstwhile playwright also conceived a magnificently malevolent vizier as a counterpart to the Mongol prince, and a stir-crazy genie as a sometime sidekick for Abu. Other differences between the two productions lie in the performances and the details. Fairbanks is really the entire show in the 1924 film; few of the other characters have any depth. The sound version, while carried by Sabu and Veidt, is marked by exceptional acting and enthusiasm down to the smallest speaking part. One example is the honey seller in Basra. He not only looks and acts the part; he also possesses the proper temperament for a Middle Eastern merchant as he barks his indignation at the trick played upon him by Abu.

As the title character, Sabu is completely in his element, running free, living by his wits and exhibiting boundless *joie de vivre*. Two constants in his character are respect for his lineage and awareness of his stomach. By way of introduction he tells Ahmad, almost bragging: "I am Abu the thief, son of Abu the thief, grandson of Abu the thief, most unfortunate of ten sons with a hunger that yawns day and night." Food is uppermost in his thoughts throughout the picture, eventually driving Ahmad to distraction. "Your eating will cause our deaths!" he cries at Abu during a moment of danger, as the youth risks their lives for a melon. "Without eating we die!" replies the ever-practical thief. Score one for Abu. Sabu also gets to sing on screen for the first time. "I Want to Be a Sailor", a jaunty tune which serves as Abu's leitmotif, is sung in a pleasing tenor by the young star. Sabu's naturalness and lack of affectation are so infectious that not even the most jaded youngster can fail to identify with him. He lived his role as Abu, he did not act it; there is not a false move in his characterization. The adolescent star had by now also lost most of his Indian accent, which had been very pronounced in *The Drum*.

Conrad Veidt seemed to draw on all his past villainous roles for his silky and sibilant interpretation of Jaffar, a magician accomplished enough to command the elements; yet when asked by the Sultan of Basra if he is a magician, he replies modestly, "I have some skill." The actor utilized his patented style of underplaying his part; Jaffar is no ranter or raver, but a supremely confident practitioner of the black arts who has everything save his love for the Princess under control. He even manages to evoke sympathy in his eternal quest for the Princess. It is when he is conjuring up storms and blinding people that he lets go, showing how inadvisable it is to upset a wicked vizier.

As King Ahmad, John Justin is certainly the most under-nourished and anemic-looking monarch ever seen on screen, yet with his fine features and cultured voice, gives a credible impersonation of a man born to the purple. His task is seemingly to stare vapidly at the Princess, although he does redeem himself at the end with some impressive swordplay. Upon completing his work on the film, Justin rushed back to Britain from America to join the Royal Air Force. There he acquitted himself bravely for the duration. He later appeared only sporadically in films, preferring to work on the stage until his death in November 2002 at the age of 85.

June Duprezs' nameless Princess is a paragon of femininity. With movements of uncommon gracefulness and a voice as soft

The Thief of Bagdad
(London Films/UA, 1940) Sabu

as spring rain added to her almond-shaped eyes and porcelain complexion, she is the perfect fairy-tale hero-ine. It is not surprising that she was not given a name, as she stands for every fictional princess who was ever cre-ated. The king, however, had to be identified, due to the close camaraderie he established with the thief. It must be admitted, though, that June appears barely alive, and her rhapsodic speech at the end of the film welcoming death can only make viewers more grateful that Sabu was around to liven things up.

The well-known John Kobal interviewed Miss Duprez a good many years later for his book *People Will Talk* (Al-fred A. Knopf, New York, 1985), which also included such diverse personalities as Anita Loos, Mae West, George Hurrell and Louise Brooks. In it June remembered the film's magnificent costumes. "They had real gold thread in them," she exulted. "Oliver Messel did them. Ohhh, at the time it was the most expensive movie ever made in Britain. And at the premier they had a statue of me wearing one of the original costumes standing out front of the cinema, looking into the pool, as in the film." As to the script: "Well, I never got a whole script all at once. It just came along in sections. And there must have been a million changes. One of my first scenes was when I was lying on the bed and the Prince [sic] comes to see her and she's in the enchanted sleep." How was it to work with the unworldly Conrad Veidt? "Veidt would never discuss anything with me anyway. I was like a little child beside him. He was simply playing his role. There was no rapport between us. Well, I was the same age as his daughter. I used to play with her (on the set); she was the only one I had to talk to."

Following her performance in *The Thief of Bagdad*, June appeared in only two more films of note, *None But The Lonely Heart* (1944) and *And Then There Were None* (1945), married a second time, raised two daughters, and retired from acting in the early fifties. She made one additional film appearance in 1961, and died in 1984 at the age of sixty-six.

As the genie able to leap tall palaces at a single bound, Rex Ingram (1895-1969) almost steals the picture, a formidable task given the personnel involved. He has the necessary élan, plus a booming, avalanche-causing laugh, not to mention the bushiest eyebrows this side of Oscar Homolka. It is his laugh, however, that gets the most play. Delivered with great gusto by Ingram at the drop of a turban, it is one of the most-remembered features of the film. This role, along with the aforementioned "De Lawd" and the part of Satan in another all-black musical, *Cabin in the Sky* (1943), are among his best performances. He continued acting up until 1968.

A stage actress noted for her precise diction, Mary Morris gives the character of Halima, Jaffar's villainous servant, a real sense of mystery and menace with her crisp voice and dark, deep-set eyes. Her dance as the murderous Silver Maid and subsequent slaying of the Sultan are achieved with chilling precision through perfect pantomime. Michael Powell's handling of this key scene harks ahead to future works of his involving dance and danger, such as *The Red Shoes* (1948) and *The Tales of Hoffmann* (1951). Miss Morris, who was born in Fiji in 1915, learned her craft at The Royal Academy of Dramatic Arts, continued her stage career, later appearing in many television productions as well, with only occasional forays into film. She died in Switzerland in 1988 at the age of 72.

Another stage personage, Morton Selten, made the most of his brief role as the Old King in the Land of Legend. With his gentle voice and kindly face, he is the personification of all the good kings found in folklore. He was seventy-nine at the time and, unfortunately, died on July 27, 1939, just days after completing his scene.

As the senile Sultan of Basra, Miles Malleson (1888-1969) paints a memorable portrait of a well-meaning parent who has his priorities confused. His mannerisms and speech pattern are reminiscent of favorite uncles the world over. Portrayed somewhat as a buffoon, he is redeemed in the desolate garden scene when he assures his daughter of his real devotion and protection. The author of numerous stage plays and screenplays, he appeared in many subsequent films before his death.

In what amounts to an extended cameo, African-

American cabaret singer Adelaide Hall (1901-1993) performs a lyrical ballad as the Princess relaxes in her garden surrounded by her handmaidens. This delightful "quiet" scene, like a slow movement in a symphony, makes the action scenes all the more appreciated and accepted.

As the long, hot days of summer 1939 dragged on, so did Ludwig Berger. Alex was at his wit's end seeking a valid reason for breaking the German director's contract. He finally realized that his ploy of hiring two other directors had not succeeded because they were working apart from Berger. What if another director were to work shoulder-to-shoulder with him? So the wily producer began co-directing Berger's scenes. That was the last straw for the distinguished doctor; he grabbed his alpenstock and took a hike. Alexander Korda, however, took no screen credit himself. He gave Berger top billing among the directors who were credited, namely, Michael Powell and Tim Whelan, although precious little of what he shot survived the final cut. In fact, Andre De Toth (1913-2002), future director of *House of Wax* (1953), in his 1994 book *Fragments - Portraits from the Inside* (Faber and Faber, London, 1994) feels that Dr. Berger made only a "halfway commitment" to direct the film, and should have been shot for what he did shoot. He also comments that "Alex Korda had taste, brilliant ideas and occasionally money."

On September 3, the day war was declared, work at Denham came to a sudden halt as cast and crew members gathered around radios to hear the awful news. Michael Powell wrapped up his work on *Thief* that day and was put in charge of a swiftly-made propaganda picture, *The Lion Has Wings* (1939). With fear of air raids and possible sabotage, production on *The Thief of Bagdad* was suspended for the time being. It resumed a month later, although the film would not be completed for another year, and then in a foreign country. More important footage remained to be shot, including Abu's and Ahmad's second reunion and the former's entry into the Land of Legend. There were also the segments that were to have been filmed in northern Africa. Since journeying anywhere in that part of the world was now out of the question, Alex Korda made arrangements for the necessary personnel to sail to America. United Artists had agreed to fund the remaining work, if done in Hollywood.

Due to wartime priorities, the move could not be made until the late spring of 1940, and it was not until almost mid-summer that work finally recommenced on *The Thief of Bagdad*. William Cameron Menzies directed a few minor shots in Hollywood while Zoltan Korda took Sabu, John Justin and June Duprez to the Grand Canyon and the Painted Desert for the necessary outdoor shots. To reach the desired level of the Grand Canyon, a team of forty mules carrying $40,000 worth of Technicolor cameras and lenses threaded its way down miles of tortuous trails led by expert cowboys and guides. It was the largest pack train ever to make the dangerous journey. Having reached their destination, the crew had to rig a cable with pulleys and sling in order to properly position the heavy equipment. This site was used as the spot Ahmad wanders into after the storm at sea, and where he is reunited with Abu. It is also where the genie takes his leave after granting Abu his final wish. The Painted Desert became the Land of Legend where Abu acquires the instruments and advice necessary to save his royal friends.

Rex Ingram's final scene, where he flies Abu to join Ahmad in the wilderness, was actually shot in a studio, where a mock-up of a section of the Grand Canyon had been constructed in proportion to the actor's exaggerated size in the film. Hornbeck's superb editing took care of the rest. Stills exist which show June Duprez with Sabu and John Justin at the Grand Canyon, but these were apparently for publicity purposes, as the Princess is in Bagdad at that point in the film's final cut.

Other deleted or altered scenes in *The Thief of Bagdad* include Abu playing dice with the Sultan's guards as a diversion, while Ahmad in the background climbs the palace wall; Abu and Ahmad escaping through the jail's corridors; the Princess being captured by bandits after her flight from Basra; Jaffar perfuming roses with a magic scent to make the Princess forget Ahmad (in the film only one rose bears the perfume); Abu being showered with arrows as he climbs the idol (no actual arrows are shot at him in the film); and Jaffar's consulting with a soothsayer. The most intriguing mystery contained in the making of this classic motion picture concerns the casket of magic pebbles which, along with a crossbow and quiver of arrows, was given to Abu by the old king in the Land of Legend. While not alluded to by the king, at least in surviving footage, it was intended that each pebble, when hurled to the ground, would spring into a warrior. This device was clearly borrowed from the silent version of *The Thief of Bagdad*, although in that picture the casket contained a magic powder that could turn into anything its owner wished.

It is eminently clear that Korda intended to use the magic pebble idea as the means through which Bagdad is retaken from Jaffar's forces. All storybooks, synopses and publicity released before the premiere mentions this ending. An example of this is the December 1940 issue of *Screen Romances*, which heralded the new film in story and photo form and includes this ending. The "pebble" ending remains in the copyrighted synopsis of the scenario that accompanied the print of the film when it was deposited at the Library of Congress on November 14, 1940, some five weeks after the sneak preview and just six weeks before its release. The mystery is deepened when the richly detailed pressbook is consulted. On the page where the making of the film was discussed, the pebbles are mentioned. On another page, which contains a column headed "The Story", the following sentences appear: "Abu finds himself in a magic valley, honored guest of a fairy King who presents him with a magic bow and arrow. The King has also a Flying Carpet and Abu steals it that night, and flies away to Bagdad." No mention of the pebbles!

Let us examine the events in the final cut of the film from the point where Abu meets the old King. The King explains about himself and his companions, then tells Abu that he is the prince with the heart of a child for whom they have been waiting "twice two thousand years." Abu is to replace him as king because "Everything is possible when seen through the eyes of youth." The old monarch next says that he will present Abu with two insignia of true kingship. He then hands Abu a quiver of arrows, followed by a crossbow. As he does this, a metal casket can clearly be seen in Abu's right hand, yet we do not see the King bestow it. Since there is a still showing the King about to hand the casket to Abu, there is obviously a deleted shot. A crossbow and arrows are but one item, since each is necessary to the other in order to function. So another gift was clearly intended. The King then tells Abu of the flying carpet but forbids him to take it, as he will need it for his trip to Paradise. Abu prays to Allah for forgiveness and takes it anyhow, placing the weapon and the casket upon it. In the ensuing flying scenes, the casket is clearly visible on the carpet. When Abu arrives in Bagdad, he fires an arrow into the executioner about to behead Ahmad, but never touches the casket.

In preparation for this book, several people were contacted in an attempt to solve this mystery. In a letter to this writer dated August 1994, Christiane Borradaile, writing for her husband, Osmond, stated: "My husband doesn't recall shooting any footage of the 'magic pebbles' - and doesn't think that any such footage was ever done." And in a phone conversation with this writer in October of 1994, Peter Ellenshaw, the assistant matte artist on the film, declared with certainty that the Bagdad palace and marketplace were not rebuilt in Hollywood, nor was any filming of the "magic pebbles" ever done. These statements suggest that the idea was scrapped after the casket was introduced but before any scenes with the warriors were shot, and that no substitute for Morton Selten could be found after his death, explaining why the casket remains in the final version. The latter part of this theory is given credence by the fact that Sabu had grown noticeably during the eighteen months involved in making the film, yet his scene with Selten, which is among those shot first and which shows a decidedly younger Sabu, was not redone.

Another factor surely was the immense pressure United Artists was under to have the problem-plagued production completed for Christmas 1940. Theaters had long been promised the film for this most profitable holiday period and were now in open revolt over the prospect of its not being available. Since it was alleged that United Artists had earlier made the statement that *The Thief of Bagdad* would be released the week of Easter 1940, serious lawsuits by exhibitors were now openly discussed. The movie's ending did not matter to the exhibitors, just as long as they had a film to show. While neither time nor money existed to recreate the mammoth Bagdad set, close-ups of Sabu sowing the magic pebbles and soldiers springing up could have been inserted into the film. In truth, it would have made the retaking of the city more believable than unarmed citizens shoving baskets over Jaffar's well-armed defenders. But with serious financial problems and fuming exhibitors, unfortunate cuts were probably mandatory. In fact, we should be thankful we have the film at all. How many other films straddled both peace and wartime, a nearly two-year shooting schedule, the moving of production to another land, and still remained so wonderfully entertaining? A German submarine did sink a cargo ship carrying a dozen copies of a sample *The Thief of Bagdad* booklet which, to establish critical U.S. copyright, had to be offered here for retail sale at ten cents each. More were provided, and these arrived safely. German submarines could have sunk a lot more, including the ships carrying the stars themselves!

With filming finally finished in late August, all that remained was the completion of the score and the editing. Both were done in time for a preview for the press the first week of October in Glendale, California. One day after the film was deposited for copyright at the Library of Congress, a request was filed by United Artists for its return. Apparently, this was when the deletions were made and the film shortened to its present length of 106 minutes. One can only wonder the extent of those deletions.

The premiere at the Carthay Circle Theatre in Los Angeles on October 17 was a glittering affair. The statue that usually stood in the fountain was temporarily replaced by larger-than-life images of June Duprez's and John Justin's characters, and a Moorish tower was added in the background. Many luminaries of the silver screen attended, including one of Sabu's favorites, Shirley Temple, who seemed quite pleased to meet "The Thief of Bagdad" in person. "Alex," reported *Screen Life* in its January 1941 issue, "provided a carpet three and one-half blocks long, extending from Wilshire Boulevard to the door of the theater, in honor of his guests. Bleachers were provided for the host of fans, and overhead searchlights played fantastically. Only in Hollywood could the fantasy of the *Arabian Nights* be duplicated." Proceeds from the five-dollar-a-ticket admission were divided equally between the Motion Picture Relief Fund and the British-American Ambulance Corps.

Following that event the long-awaited Arabian Nights extravaganza was road shown for several weeks at prestige theaters across the country. *The Thief of Bagdad* went into general release in the U.S. on Christmas Day 1940. In Britain it was shown to the Trade on December 24, but did not go into general release until March 10, 1941. No finer gift could have been given to the film-going public by St. Nicholas himself. A film of the ages for all ages, *The Thief of Bagdad* captured the dreamlike mood of the legendary *Arabian Nights* better than any other motion picture and remains unsurpassed even today. Viewing it is still a wonderful experience, especially for those adept at suspending their disbelief. Not without reason is it subtitled "An Arabian Fantasy". Among other things this notifies the viewer to expect a heightened richness of language and exalted viewpoint of romance.

One brilliantly realized sequence is designed especially to touch the viewer, the scene where Ahmad first meets the Princess in the garden of the Sultan's palace:

Princess: "Where have you come from?"

Ahmad: "From the other side of time, to find you."

Princess: "How long have you been searching?"

Ahmad: "Since time began."

Princess: "Now that you have found me, how long will you stay?"

Ahmad: "Till the end of time. For me, there is no more beauty in the world but yours."

To those living in a world despoiled by war, such a concept may have been hard to accept, but it sounded believable once you got into the swing of things.

The spirit of adventure has never been better personified than Abu's stirring words of encouragement to the despondent Ahmad in the famous dungeon scene: "We'll take a boat, go down to the sea. I've never seen the sea, but I've heard the sailors on the riverside talk about it. The sea; with fishes as big as the Great Temple and little ones as tiny as my little finger, with wings, and boats as big as Bagdad itself, with sails as big as clouds and when the wind blows, they go as fast as antelopes and carry you to the isles of India and China!"

And Jaffar's tortured baring of his soul when his one desire to hold the Princess in his arms has been thwarted: "I have powers that could force you to my will, but I want more than they can give. I want your love. Forget Ahmad. He is no longer blind. For men with eyes, the world is full of women. Only I am cursed, that I can see only you!" One can revel in the sheer poetry of the film's magnificent dialogue as well as its rapturous music, stunning sets, sublime photography, and heroic story, all of which lend intensity to the memorable acting. Few other films ever offered such cascading words of poetry as when the diminutive thief, firmly clasping the genie's hair, fearfully asks where they are flying to, and receives the following reply in a crescendo of soaring music - "To the Roof of the World...Supported by seven pillars, and the seven pillars are set on the shoulders of a genie whose strength is beyond thought, and the genie stands on an eagle, and the eagle on a bull, and the bull on a fish, and the fish SWIMS in the sea of eternity!"

Nor does the script lack for humor. While in his canine state, Abu is deprecatingly referred to by a merchant as a "frequenter of tree trunks". When the clever animal selects a false coin from among a handful, the same man exclaims: "This is no dog, but the reincarnation of a tax collector!" When the sultan shows his toy collection to Jaffar, he explains: "I do prefer these things to my subjects...so often my subjects fail to do what I want and then I have to have their heads cut off." Told his collection is only "near completion," he indignantly sputters that his collection is of the "most complete completion."

In another sequence Abu and Ahmad, reduced to poverty, are dismissed by a turbaned gentleman with the words: "Allah be with you, but I doubt it." When Abu realizes his fellow prisoner really is the king, he prostrates himself and begs to be left "with one arm for small stealing." Later, when his newfound friend realizes that he must see the love of his life one more time, Abu, with typical boyish derision, scornfully says: "Aw, I know all about that." At the end of the film, when apparently Abu's reward for saving everyone is a chance to go to school, the lad gasses up the flying carpet in record time and immediately takes off. Waving goodbye, he cries that his goal now is "for some fun and adventure at last!" If fighting giant spiders, being stepped on by a towering genie, shipwrecked at sea, trapped in the Temple of the Dawn, and changed into a dog did not constitute adventure to the lad, one can only wonder what did.

The film is also a visual feast. For instance; Jaffar's ship sweeping with billowing sails into the bustling harbor at Basra (actually all done with wind machines and moving camera; the ship itself was stationary) the flock of white birds flying overhead, which is the first sight seen by Ahmad when he regains his vision; the procession of the Princess in the marketplace; the genie rising from the bottle; and Abu's fearfully holding onto the genie as they fly over the Roof of the World. Added to these images is the full eight-minute sequence comprising Abu's entry into the Temple of the Dawn, his surreal battle with the giant spider, his encounter with the blue-skinned guardians of the idol, and his theft of the ruby eye from the forehead of the Goddess. In fact, the only sounds intruding upon the proceedings are of Abu nervously whistling and singing "I Want to Be a Sailor" while he strides along the winding chasms of the temple complex, and the anguished chant the guardians begin when Abu removes the gem from the giant, shadowed image. "Not for two thousand years will she grow another!" cries the genie in admiration when Abu proudly shows his prize to him.

Miklos Rozsa's lyrical score beautifully underlines the action with its combination of orchestral instruments, singing and chants adding immeasurably to the viewer's enjoyment. His music perfectly conveys the varied moods of the complex storyline with consummate skill, beginning with the opening fanfare that alerts the viewer to the spectacle about to commence. There is scarcely a moment in the film where Rozsa's music does not add to the drama or the pleasure. It is constantly present: sweeping, inspiring, exalting, probing and dipping deep into our emotions. Without it the film is nothing; with it, it is everything. Try imagining *Gone with the Wind* without the score. Steiner's booming "Tara's Theme" told more of Scarlett's love for the land and her birthright than any words or photography could. Try imagining *The Thief of Bagdad* without its score. It would be like coming across a fountain devoid of water in a desert oasis. Everywhere in the film the music skips and dances, leading the viewer like a Pied Piper on to greater expectations. Seldom has the drama and action of a major motion picture been so closely synthesized with its score to combine into a completely integrated and unique experience.

Author and film lecturer Rudy Behlmer reports in his book *Behind the Scenes - The Making of 16 Classic Hollywood Films* (Samuel French, 1990) that *The Thief of Bagdad* was the first true showcase for the extraordinary film talents of Miklos Rozsa. He states the music "is really foreground rather than background music and literally sweeps the film along." He further records that Rosza's "vibrant, singing lyricism was superbly demonstrated in 'The Love of the Princess,' in which the two love themes associated with the Princess and Ahmad were intertwined."

All of the music for *The Thief of Bagdad* was composed after the film was completed, with the exception of two sequences: the Old Sultan on the Flying Horse and the Dance of the Silver Maid and the songs utilizing Sir Robert Vansittart's lyrics. For these the music was composed earlier, based upon descriptions in the script.

Like all films, *The Thief of Bagdad* is not perfect, and has its detractors. Some find it slow, and some find its plotline a bit tortuous what with its early flashback scene and cutting from character to character. It is an odd combination of languid drowsy love combined with spirited action. It's almost archaic language from *The Arabian Nights* is a far cry from the derring-do in the historical epics of Errol Flynn. One should bring no preconceptions to *The Thief of Bagdad*; one should accept it only as it is. It did have flaws, however. The model of the flying genie was really no better than the offerings of matinee serials at the time. A storyline mix-up occurs when the Sultan informs Jaffar he has only one daughter, and a few moments later the Princess informs her handmaiden that she will flee to her sister who has married the Sultan of Samarkand. Maybe the old Sultan meant he had only one daughter available. Jaffar had only moments before movingly said of his vision of the Princess: "Her eyes are Babylonian eyes," and after reveling in that kind of language, who cares about genealogy?

Subsequent to the Korda film, there have been two remakes of *The Thief of Bagdad*. One was a 1961 French-Italian production which starred muscleman Steve Reeves and was directed by Arthur Lubin (who had earlier been a key personality in Sabu's career). This version was conceived and received as a juvenile-oriented action picture. Noted film historian Leonard Maltin terms it "occasionally atmospheric, but nothing like the Sabu version." The year 1978 saw a British-French re-filming which was shown on television in the United States and in theaters abroad. It employed the considerable talents of Peter Ustinov and Roddy McDowall, and Maltin correctly terms it an "adventure that's handsome enough, but nowhere near the definitive 1940 version."

Dr. Josef Goebbels, Adolf Hitler's Minister of Propaganda and head of Nazi Germany's film production, saw Korda's *The Thief of Bagdad* and vowed the "Herrenvolk" could do as well or better. In the midst of crushing wartime privations he marshaled Germany's entire film industry for a monumental filming of the much-beloved Teutonic tales of Baron Munchausen. Called *Munchausen*, it opened in 1943 and was the first movie to utilize the Agfacolor process. With a cast of thousands and footage filmed as far away as Venice, Italy, it proved a feast for the eyes and a decided tonic for war-weary patrons. Its sets showed definite inspiration derived from *The Thief of Bagdad*, as does its magnificent costumes and use of color. Even its score can be compared to some of the more serious portions of Rozsa's music. But the story featured no Princess and no young thief, no lovesick king or evil vizier. In places it was awe-inspiring, but it had no soul. Technically perfect, it lacked a story in which one could become involved. Even Dr. Goebbels, who knew a thing or two about stirring up the masses, was defeated on this one. *Munchausen* was a real achievement, but it was as cold as the winter battle fronts in Russia. Korda's *Thief* still reigned supreme.

It must have been something to have seen *The Thief of Bagdad* during the darkest days of World War II, when death rained down from the skies. For it was during the period of the famous Battle of Britain and its attendant Nazi blitz intended to terrorize the people into capitulation, that the movie opened. Screenings were often suspended when air raid sirens jolted audiences back from Korda's world of make-believe and caused them to grope their way to the nearest underground tube for shelter. How must it have been to resurface to a world in flames and perhaps even the theater they had so recently vacated, a mound of rubble? How easy was it to return to the soothing fantasies and juvenile evils of Korda's epic when the sounds and smells of war seeped through the very walls of the theaters themselves? For at this time a far more sinister figure than Jaffar was looming across the channel, and Britain and her empire stood alone.

While people queued up for blocks in London and the provinces to see the wonder the imaginative Korda had prepared for them, critics everywhere were ecstatic over his cinematic spectacle and urged everyone to see it. This is particularly exemplified by Bosley Crowther's review in

The New York Times: "The color alone makes this picture a truly exciting entertainment. But, so, too, do the performances of Sabu, the Indian boy, as the little thief, or Conrad Veidt as the turbaned Grand Vizier with eyes of amazing potency...." A few critics were less than gracious regarding certain of the film's elements, but all agreed on the superiority of the color and the fine performances of Sabu and Conrad Veidt. A good example of an ambivalent review is that which appeared in *Variety*: "*The Thief of Bagdad* is one of the most colorful and eye-appealing spectacles ever screened. It's an expensive production accenting visual appeal, combining sweeping panoramas and huge sets, amazing special effects and process photography, and the most vividly magnificent Technicolor yet." Still, the reviewer complained that the film contained numerous scenes that ran too long. He ended with the contradictory view that "Conrad Veidt is most impressive as the sinister grand vizier, sharing honors with Sabu, who capably carries off the title role," yet stated: "On both the acting and directing side, the picture is obviously deficient."

Korda himself, in an interview after the film's release, explained his purpose in producing the film. "Since the talkies came in, fantasy has been virtually unknown on the screen. The Walt Disney cartoons have kept it alive almost alone. In the excitement over Disney's excesses, most of us forgot that he was teaching us a lesson, or, at the least, reminding us of what we had lost. I, for one, took that reminder to heart. That is why I have produced *The Thief of Bagdad.*" Korda's curious use of the word "excesses" may be an acknowledgement that Disney's *Snow White*, when first released in England a few years back, had received an equivalent of our "Parental Guidance" rating for fear children would be upset by its darker scenes.

When all was said and done, the film did exceptionally well at the box office, and its technical excellence was acknowledged by the Academy of Motion Picture Arts and Sciences with three awards: Best Cinematography (Color), Best Art Direction (Color), and Best Special Effects. Miklos Rozsa's brilliant score also received a nomination, but the winners that year for Best Original Score were Leigh Harline, Paul J. Smith, and Ned Washington for the Disney animated feature *Pinocchio*. Rozsa did receive a sort of honorary award when the "Djinn's Flight Theme" was utilized as the melody for "High Flight," a popular wartime aviator song.

Noted film writer Leonard Maltin wonders "if a so-called professional actor could have achieved what Sabu did in *The Thief of Bagdad*. Sabu's wonderful naiveté was just right for the role of the thief, and he made it his own." "One remarkable thing about Sabu," Maltin continues, "is that he never seemed to be acting. Whether he was saying corny dialogue in one of those Universal potboilers, or playing the privileged prince in *Black Narcissus,* he always seemed sincere and genuine. I think that was his great gift: he was a natural."

While not an original story like *King Kong*, *The Thief of Bagdad* ranks high on the list of great fantasy films. Containing all the necessary elements for one, it goes one step further in properly combining those elements into a superior whole. The end result was a motion picture to which all who were involved could point with great pride. While most film buffs may agree that silent and sound versions of movies should not be compared, it is safe to say that the 1940 remake of the 1924 *The Thief of Bagdad* is at least equal to, if not superior to, its predecessor. Even without its dialogue, Korda's production is on a visual par with the Fairbanks' film. And thanks to the miracle of modern technology, it will always be around to take viewers on a magic carpet ride whenever they so desire.

With *The Thief of Bagdad*, Sabu reached his pinnacle. Few film personalities had come so far so fast. His "rags-to-riches" story, going from earning less than a dollar a month to being the star of his very first movie, surpassed in unbelievability even the magic carpet ride he took in his third film. Most other movie stars first had a career on stage or in radio or vaudeville, or began as bit players or were given exploratory roles in "B" productions. Sabu was almost alone in starting at the top. And what is more important, he remained on top for one more marvelous production. If his career was due to falter, it was not apparent from the next project slated for him, for that was *Jungle Book*.

Chapter Six

America and Hollywood

Arriving in Hollywood in mid-1940 with the other cast members needed for the remaining scenes of *The Thief of Bagdad*, Sabu found himself in another Land of Legend. There in sunny Southern California were all the biggest names in the film industry of the day, for Hollywood was then, as now, the center of all things cinematic. Its numerous studios were creating some of their finest films. The previous year had seen the release of *Gone with the Wind*, *The Wizard of Oz*, and *Stagecoach*, to name but a few. The present year had already yielded *The Grapes of Wrath*, *His Girl Friday* and *Rebecca*. Box-office returns were growing as the nation began to see the light at the end of the tunnel of the decade-long Great Depression.

Prosperity was beginning to rear its beautiful head. America's massive rearmament program and sales to a war-torn Europe were providing jobs for the chronically unemployed, but the loss of foreign receipts due to the fighting had begun to have a dampening effect upon studio budgets and optimistic production plans. None of the glamour of the film capital adversely affected the young Indian, however. Always very practical and realistic, Sabu was well aware that his time in the sun could be short-lived, and he intended to enjoy his fame and fortune while it lasted. If he ever did forget this, his brother Dastagir was there to remind him. His older sibling had been looking after him ever since the two brothers had left their homeland for England. Just a little over a year after the pair's arrival on American shores, he became Sabu's business manager, a position he would hold until a year after his younger brother's marriage.

With the long-awaited premiere of *The Thief of Bagdad* finally behind him in mid-October, the adolescent actor returned to New York briefly to appear in Louella Parson's *Hollywood on Broadway* revue, which opened at Loew's State Theater, where it ran from October 24 through October 30. The variety piece showcased the talents of promising newcomers to filmdom, among them Ilona Massey, Robert Stack, Brenda Joyce, Patricia Morison, Binnie Barnes, William Orr and Mike Frankovich. Sabu's contribution to the proceedings was a spirited rendition of "I Want to Be a Sailor" from his soon-to-be-released motion picture. In a letter to this writer received in September 1994, Robert Stack (1919-2003) recalled Sabu as "...a very pleasant young man [who] fascinated all the pretty girls...

He was truly the Romeo of the Louella Parsons tour." Sabu continued with the company until United Artists sent him on their own tour of personal appearances for *Thief* openings in a number of important cities, during which he was accompanied by "Princess" June Duprez, traveling about in an airplane appropriately dubbed *The Flying Carpet*.

By early 1941, with those attendant personal appearances for *Thief* out of the way, Sabu found that there was much to interest him in the Land of Liberty. He discovered that his passion for fast cars could be gratified easily in California, where dragsters and drag strips abounded. Often improvised on local thoroughfares, the latter were no less fun for that fact. Sabu leaped at the chance of participating in the popular races after passing his driving test on his first attempt. When not behind the wheel of his dragster, Sabu could be seen driving either his Ford station wagon or his Buick convertible.

It was in the United States that the young celebrity really showed his adaptability. After four years in conservative England, with its class system and rigid traditions being his introduction to western civilization (not to mention those he had experienced in hidebound India), he was able to fit right into the liberal atmosphere of swing era America. Possessed of a genuine love for humanity, he made friends as easily in the U.S. as he had in Britain and soon considered the comparatively young nation his home. Sabu's natural warmth, quick smile, and above-average intelligence were the keys to his social success. Finding many aspects of American life to his liking, the attraction became mutual. Soon the young film star became a fixture on the local scene; when not indulging his love of ice cream in some malt shop or roasting hot dogs on the beach, he could be found swimming, boxing or wrestling at the Hollywood Athletic Club or racing on one of the aforementioned drag strips. Sabu would also avail himself of the advantages open to one in his position. He would spend a day at the racetrack with fellow actor Leo Gorcey of "The East Side Kids", and take out movie starlets, frequently double-dating with his good friend Bud Knight, who recalls him as "a regular guy". He gave autographs freely, always with a smile. Occasionally meeting with a biased remark because of his dark complexion, he would ignore it rather than create a scene. Sabu's ties to America were further strengthened when his brother married an American girl, Betty Swing, the daughter of an Army general. Dastagir, who was called "Shaik" by his friends, lived in a comfortable house on Curzon Street in Hollywood which he shared with Sabu.

For three days in April 1941, Sabu was part of a contingent of Hollywood stars who volunteered to appear at the Motion Picture Festival being held in Mexico City. Among those who accompanied the popular young personality to this important event were Laurel and Hardy, Norma Shearer, Wallace Beery and Patricia Morison. Not a typical

Hollywood junket designed to promote current movies, it was, rather, a delegation of friendship to all countries south of the border, basically under President Roosevelt's new "Good Neighbor" policy. Huge crowds turned out wherever the Americans appeared.

Alex Korda had also remained in the film capital after the premiere of *The Thief of Bagdad*. He kept busy the only way he knew how - by creating new motion pictures. (There has been much speculation over the years of Korda's involvement with the British Secret Service prior to and during the war, but that remains unsubstantiated.) He produced and directed a lavish historical drama, *That Hamilton Woman* (1941), starring Vivien Leigh and Laurence Olivier, a motion picture intended to help keep England fighting Hitler. Prime Minister Winston Churchill reportedly watched this film many times, proclaiming it his favorite movie. Alex then produced the highly romantic *Lydia* (1941) for his wife, Merle Oberon. He also procured the monies necessary to begin the filming of Ernst Lubitsch's dark comedy *To Be or Not to Be* (1942), and was acknowledged by having his old Big Ben logo with the words "Alexander Korda Presents" run at the film's opening. Even while engaged on these projects, his nimble mind was thinking well ahead. Before *Lydia* was released in September the call went out, and Sabu found himself reporting for work on yet another movie set.

Chapter Seven

Jungle Book

It has often been said that certain actors are born to play certain roles. This was never truer than in the case of Sabu's portraying Mowgli, the feral protagonist of Rudyard Kipling's most enduring works, *The Jungle Book* and *The Second Jungle Book*. Being Indian, he possessed the proper ethnicity and, with his handsome features and athletic physique, made a most attractive wild boy. At seventeen, he was the age attained by Mowgli in the last of the stories, which made him a bit old for the earlier tales, but no one complained.

When noted British author Aldous Huxley, who was then working in Hollywood on film scenarios, suggested the idea of filming the famous jungle tales to Alex Korda in mid-1941, the grateful producer quickly gathered his brothers around him and began planning a production of *Jungle Book*. Kipling's inspiration for the tales was his own short story from his 1893 collection *Many Inventions*. Entitled "In the Rukh", it tells of a boy raised by wolves. According to his autobiography, *Something of Myself*, he combined that idea with childhood memories of Masonic Lions and a phrase from his friend H. Rider Haggard's novel *Nada the Lily* to create *The Jungle Books*. To adapt the stories into a workable screenplay, Alex Korda hired Laurence Stallings (1894-1968), the World War I veteran who had co-authored the famed anti-war play *What Price Glory?* with Maxwell Anderson and gone on to script many films.

The rest of the technicians had all worked for Korda on previous films - William Hornbeck as editor, Lawrence Butler on special effects, Miklos Rozsa as composer of the score, Academy Award-winner Lee Garmes (1898-1978), who had lensed *Lydia*, as cinematographer, and of course, Zoltan as director and Vincent as art director.

In July the production crew was dispatched to Lake Sherwood, an extensive and picturesque wooded region some twenty miles north of Los Angeles. There, on a ten-acre site, a complete and habitable village was built. Among its occupants were Rosemary DeCamp, who played Messua, Mowgli's true mother; Jerome Cowan as Buldeo the hunter; Patricia O'Rourke as his daughter Mahala; Frank Puglia as a pundit; John Qualen as the village barber; and Ralph Byrd as a villager friendly to Messua. Also along for the ride was a pair of Bengal tigers named Rajah and Rose. They would take turns playing Shere Khan, Mowgli's arch enemy. Nissa, the leopard that had appeared in *Bringing Up Baby* (1938), was also on hand. Besides these name-bearing animals were twenty-two female elephants, five black panthers, one bear, many deer, scores of monkeys, several wolves and wolf cubs, a small herd of water buffalo, numerous sheep and goats, one small dog, and a horse that had two hooves in the glue factory. The rest of the filming was done at the General Services Studio in Los Angeles.

During filming, it was these non-union cast members who received most of the press. More than one scribe recorded how the wolves fought among themselves, the black panthers fought with all the other animals, and how the monkeys broke loose and all but moved into the nearby neighborhoods. Readers learned from magazine and newspaper articles why five black panthers were needed to portray Bagheera (they are extremely vicious and cannot be trained), how the elephants almost stampeded during the jungle fire sequence, and how trainer Louis Roth kept his tigers in line (with a bamboo cane and baby talk). Nor was that all. With the original Bagheera having died of old age before filming began, a second black panther was given the role. This replacement was obviously much younger, for it grabbed a prop man by the arm and dragged him onto a tree limb. The man, who had mercifully fainted, was only saved by Louis Roth's expertise. While second-unit director Andre De Toth diverted the carnivore's attention with a slab of meat, Roth grabbed the prop man's body as it dropped and carried him to safety.

Meanwhile, Alex Korda was learning the hard way that Great Danes do not make good substitutes for tigers. One of those noble canines having been tested as a tiger unsuccessfully, a real 550-pound Bengal cat was brought in to portray Shere Khan. This was unbeknownst to the producer, who stepped into its cage one day while the beast was being filmed. Roth was also present as Korda made some unwise gestures toward the big cat. The trainer finally prevailed upon the producer to leave; as he did so, the tiger leapt after him. Fortunately, the door closed outward, and the animal hit the back of it. The sight of it towering over him caused Korda to faint, however. When he awoke a few minutes later, he again fainted at the sight of the tiger looming so near.

Sabu probably found all the attention directed toward the animals gratifying, given his remarkable rapport with four-legged creatures. Besides the elephants, the wolves were very chummy with him, and he rode the water buffalo as if he had been born atop one. For insurance and safety reasons, however, Sabu's scenes with the panthers and tigers had to be filmed with glass separating man from beast. While a real python portrayed Kaa in his introductory shot, a rubber likeness which moved by wires controlled by a team of prop men was used for the scenes in which the creature appears with Mowgli. The king cobra in the treasure chamber sequence was achieved in the same manner. Rounding out the reptilian contingent was a mechanical crocodile. Baloo the bear, although introduced at the beginning of the story, was not seen again, a victim of the editor's shears. Of the fifteen tales comprising the two books, eight deal with Mowgli. From these, Stallings selected five: "Mowgli's Brothers", "Tiger! Tiger!", "How Fear Came", "Letting in the Jungle" and "The King's Ankus", while borrowing just one line of dialogue from "The Spring Running", and the word for the Hunting People ("We be of one blood, ye and I") from "Kaa's Hunting". Buldeo, a character who appears in the second and fourth of the aforementioned stories, is seen in the film's framing segments as an old man relating his account of Mowgli's life to an audience of Indians and a young English woman.

The first-named tale tells of Mowgli's adoption by a wolf pack when, as an infant, he wanders into the cave of a family of wolves. It then skips ahead a decade and tells how Mowgli and Bagheera the Black Panther became friends. Also related is the boy's enmity with Shere Khan the Tiger, and its exacerbation at a meeting of the jungle animals. Most of the latter side with Shere Khan and drive Mowgli from the jungle.

The next, "Tiger! Tiger!", is concerned with Mowgli's first contact with men and of his settling his score with Shere Khan. He journeys to a village far from the jungle where he is given a home by the richest woman, whose infant son had been taken by a tiger. She hopes Mow-gli might be her child, but soon decides he is not. She teaches him her language and he becomes the village herd-boy. Some months later, Mowgli gets an opportunity to kill Shere Khan. With the help of two wolves, he maneuvers the water buffalo herd into trapping the big cat in a ravine where it is trampled to death.

"How Fear Came" includes the origin of the tiger's stripes and a drought which nearly destroys all the jungle flora and fauna.

In the fourth story, "Letting in the Jungle", Mowgli returns to the wolf-pack. One day he overhears Buldeo speaking with some villagers and learns that Messua and her husband have been accused of harboring a devil-child. The couple is tied up in their home, awaiting death by fire. Mowgli frees them, then returns again to the jungle where he organizes the animals and leads them toward the village in an effort to drive out the humans by destroying their homes and crops.

The final tale, "The King's Ankus", relates the visit of Mowgli and Kaa the python to the treasure chamber of an ancient king in a long-dead city. Guarded by a superannuated cobra, the treasure includes an ankus (elephant goad) containing a priceless ruby and encrusted with turquoise which alone of all the items Mowgli finds attractive. Warned by the cobra that the ankus will bring death, Mowgli takes it anyhow. Tiring of it, he leaves it in the jungle. Later, finding that a man has taken it, he follows the trail, and discovers six dead men before locating the goad. While he knows that they had killed one another for posses-

Jungle Book (United Artists, 1942) Sabu

sion of the ankus, he does not understand why.

Stallings utilized the beginning of the first tale up to the point where Mowgli reaches his pre-teen years and vows to kill Shere Khan. All of "Tiger! Tiger!" is drawn upon, with some alterations. In the film Messua is widowed early on, as her husband is killed by a tiger while searching for their infant son who had wandered into the jungle. Buldeo is, of course, a younger man in this extended flashback, and has a daughter who becomes a sort of pseudo-love interest for Mowgli. Mowgli kills Shere Khan single-handedly with a knife after luring the big cat into a river, although this does not occur until much later in the film.

Little of "How Fear Came" is used; Buldeo's narration at the beginning tells how the tiger got its stripes, and the drought is replaced by a fire which occurs at the end of the picture. Here the screenplay alternates events from the final two stories along with other changes. Mahala replaces Kaa as Mowgli's companion in the treasure chamber sequence and Mowgli heeds the cobra's warning about the ankus and takes nothing with him, although the girl leaves with one gold coin. When her father sees it, she tells him of the city and he immediately begins scheming. He is forced to confide in the pundit and the barber; the trio fills in for Kipling's unnamed and faceless men of greed.

It is then in Stallings' story that Mowgli gets his chance to settle with Shere Khan. He goes off alone; Messua, frantic, trusts in Buldeo and his cronies to bring him back. Mowgli, with some assistance from Kaa, is victorious over the tiger. Buldeo tries to force him to tell him the location of the lost city, but with Bagheera's aid the boy makes the hunter believe that he can change into a panther at will and chases the man back to the village. There Buldeo condemns Mowgli as a witch; the boy is bound and whipped. The hunter allows Messua to help Mowgli escape so that he can lead him and the others to the treasure chamber. He then has Messua tied up as an accomplice before following Mowgli, who deliberately leads the men to the city, remembering the old cobra's words. Sure enough, the pundit kills the barber and is in turn taken by a crocodile. Buldeo alone survives and returns to the village, filled with vengeance. At the same time, Mowgli is headed for the village leading a herd of elephants. Buldeo drives a wagon full of flaming hay into the jungle in an attempt to burn out Mowgli and the jungle creatures. The wind shifts, however, and the fire heads toward the village, forcing the villagers to flee their homes. Mowgli forgets his idea when he meets them; Mahala informs him of Messua's peril and he goes to rescue her. Once assured of her safety, he begins aiding the animals trapped by the fire. Messua and Mahala watch him from an island in mid-stream. Messua calls to Mowgli to come back with her, but he shakes his head and says, "I am of the jungle; their lair is my lair; their trail is my trail; their fight is my fight." He turns and enters the jungle. Back in the present, the English woman asks Buldeo what became of Mowgli and the others. The now-mellowed hunter smiles and replies, "That, *memsahib*, is another story."

As well as adhering very closely to Kipling's storyline, Stallings retained the language of the jungle creatures, such as "red flower" for fire, "man-pack" for humans and "tooth" for knife. The writer also used some of the dialogue nearly verbatim; for example, the single line lifted from "The Spring Running", spoken by Messua the last time she sees Mowgli: "But it is no longer my son. It is a godling of the forest! Ahai!" (Kipling); "Ahai! He is no longer my son. He is a godling of the forest!" (Stallings). A slight alteration, to be sure, but still a difference. The scenarist reserves most of the comic relief for the trio of villagers in their greedy search for and discovery of the treasure, but bits of humor crop up elsewhere as well, such as Messua's dog growling at Mowgli as the boy laps up water from her well, and receiving a growl from the youth in return. Stallings' treatment of Kipling's renowned books really leaves nothing to be desired, as he selected the most interesting aspects of the much-loved stories to bring to life on the silver screen. And he does so in a very entertaining fashion, with the accent on action and a minimum of dialogue.

The overall look of the film was a compromise between Alex and Zoltan, with the producer preferring a glossy look while the director wanted realism. So the youngest brother, Vincent, who had no say in the matter, used designs based on southeast Asian architecture for his temples and village, and spray-painted the leaves on the trees in homage to the great god Technicolor. Some $48,000 worth of tropical plants was also utilized to appease any botanists who might be among the viewers. The lower portions of enormous tropical trees were constructed by the art department and the upper portions were added through the use of matte paintings. The lost city sets were enhanced with matte paintings and miniatures. The result is very beautiful, with white deer leaping gracefully before a tapestry of multi-hued jungle flora and blue and gray temples rising against an azure sky. Even the destructive fire is a thing of beauty in Vincent Korda's wonderfully creative hands.

To fill up the treasure chamber in the dead city, Alex Korda bought 70,000 coins struck for the 1939-40 Golden Gate International Exposition held in San Francisco. On

screen they look
like a million, piled
in glistening heaps
upon the dusty
stone floor.

Miklos Rozsa
contributed one of
his most notable
scores for *Jungle
Book*, this time us-

Jungle Book (United Artists, 1942)
Patricia O'Rourke, Sabu - Photo
Courtesy of the Margaret Herrick Library

ing leitmotifs for the various animals and the stylings
of authentic Indian ragas for the Hindu scenes. For the
main part of the film, the composer wrote characteristic
and diatonic music. The remainder of the music creates
a wonderfully exotic mood for this timeless tale of Indian
life and legend. He also composed a song, "Jungle's Lullaby", with lyrics by Arthur Wimperis, which is sung over
one scene and used as Messua's theme. In the year following the film's release, Rozsa recorded *The Jungle Book
Suite* in New York with the NBC Symphony Orchestra for
the RCA Victor label, and narration by Sabu (at Rozsa's
insistence), making it the first commercial recording for
a dramatic film. (Disney's *Snow White* had its soundtrack
songs issued as an album in late 1937 or early 1938.) A
symphonic version of the score was created and occasionally played by symphony orchestras of the period. It is
worthy of note that this suite was included at the first con-

cert Rozsa conducted at the Hollywood Bowl in 1943. This was the fourth among sixteen of Rozsa's scores to garner an Academy Award nomination over a forty-six-year span. He won the golden statuette for *Spellbound* (1945), *A Double Life* (1947) and *Ben-Hur* (1959).

The composer recalled an amusing encounter during filming, in his autobiography *Double Life*. It was his first meeting with Sabu, who presented Rozsa with a sure-fire scheme for solving their financial woes. The two would collaborate on a stage act wherein the actor would sing songs composed by Rozsa while riding an elephant. Informed that an orchestra would be too costly, Sabu savvily told Rozsa to offer the musicians half the going rate.

Lee Garmes' camera work is superb, presenting the viewer with a number of unforgettable images. Among them are Mowgli riding the great water buffalo, and the long shot of Mowgli and Mahala being welcomed into the jungle by the wolf pack.

According to Rosemary DeCamp's vastly entertaining audio book, *Tales from Hollywood*, the making of *Jungle Book* was largely a comedy of errors. The actress recalls: "George and Gordon Bau, two talented and inventive makeup men, had evolved a new stain to color all of us the same shade for the erratic and inconsistent Technicolor film of that period. The big crowd scenes, which were to be filmed first, involved every principal in the story, as well as a lot of extras. Central Casting had sent a hundred or so assorted Hindus, Muslims, Sikhs, Touchables and Un-touchables, with no regard or awareness of their religious differences. These were to surface later into mayhem.

"The first four days everyone seemed to get along. They were dressed in unbleached cotton singlets and dhotis...for pants. Then everyone was stained with the new makeup, regardless of sex, color, or whatever. The margin for error in those early years of color was widened by the inability of the lab to get the 'rushes' or 'dailies' processed and returned in less than four days. The assistant director broke the news to the Bau Brothers at 6 a.m. on the fifth day that it all had to be done over because wherever the men had perspired, the makeup had turned their body fluids bright green in Technicolor. To the naked eye the moisture had just appeared as natural sweat. I wish I could have heard the commotion when those first scenes were run in the projection room. All those 'natives' flapping around with green groins and armpits must have been a sensation...especially at, say, a thousand dollars a foot."

DeCamp continues: "Meanwhile the Muslims, Hindus and Sikhs were chasing each other with knives after dinner. The screams of the aggressors and the wounded became a nightly lullaby. The Kordas went home to sleep, so they did not realize how our little war was hotting up, until one wild night a leaping Sikh threw his curved sword at a Hindu. Lives were spared, but the weapon overturned some candles and the big restaurant tent burned to the ground."

The crowning mishap occurred on a day which saw the river set crowded with agents, financiers, casual onlookers, crew members and most of the cast. That particular set held three feet of water, underneath which ran the track used to propel the rubber python. A small group of elephants was to proceed to the edge of the river and stop there. However, the beasts had been suffering so much from the heat that they did not stop. The leader tripped over the underwater track and fell on her side; the others soon followed suit. The resulting mini-tsunami bowled over most of the audience with either water or laughter. The pachyderms were oblivious to the pandemonium they had caused, being too busy spraying water over their parched hides.

Principal photography was finished by the end of October, but the scene in which Messua and Mahala take refuge from the fire on a small island had to be re-shot. As Ms. DeCamp states in her book: "In early winter, when we had assumed *Jungle Book* was finished and on its way to the theaters, I got a telegram saying, 'Are you available to work in water November 21st? (Signed) Korda.' That odd language is practical contractualese for female performers.... This time the lagoon had been rebuilt in a giant tank at General Service Studios in Hollywood. It was smaller and deeper with a little sandy island in the middle. Sir Alex Korda was directing by bullhorn. Zoltan was nowhere in sight. I was made up, dressed in my old sari, and told to wade in and make for the island. The water was waist-deep and chilly. There were huge fans blowing red powder so that the air looked fiery and the water reflected orange light. The effect was marvelously colorful. The whole sky and forest seemed to be burning up..."

It is not known if Sabu ever read *The Jungle Books*, although he may very well have done so at Beaconstone, but his rendering of Mowgli's dialogue and his reactions to strange new things show a clear understanding of the character. Once again he carried a film, not because he had so much screen time, but because he *was* the character he portrayed. By his physical presence alone, Sabu dominates this film as he does no other, making *Jungle Book* the quintessential Sabu movie. In only her third film, Rosemary DeCamp (1910-2001) gives a moving performance as a woman who has lost both husband and child. She made a career of playing mothers, although she was seldom old enough to be a parent to the actor portraying her child. Such is the case here, as she was only fourteen years older than Sabu. Her gentle look and soothing voice were no doubt the reasons for this typecasting. She is probably best remembered as the nurse on the popular *Dr. Christian* radio show, a role she played for seventeen years. She also appeared on the small screen at its inception in *The Life of Riley* starring Jackie Gleason, achieving much success there as well. Younger fans will recall her as

Marlo Thomas' mother on the *That Girl* series of the late '60s and early '70s.

When Jerome Cowan had to bow out of his role for personal reasons, he was replaced by the always-reliable Joseph Calleia (1897-1975), who gives a fine performance as Buldeo the hunter. He is especially convincing as the older Buldeo, the younger one being akin to the gangsters he usually played. Born on Malta, the actor had had a successful radio and stage career in England before emigrating to the United States. Patricia O'Rourke (b. 1927), who played Mahala, Mowgli's apparently platonic love interest, was the only novice among the major players. The fourteen-year-old high-school student had been discovered by no less a personage than Alexander Korda. She was one-half Hawaiian by descent, giving her the necessary touch of exoticism. *Jungle Book* seems to have been her first and only film, as she has vanished from sight. As Buldeo's cohorts, Frank Puglia (1892-1975) and John Qualen (1899-1987) provided competent support. Puglia, a Sicilian with a background in opera, had been in films since the early twenties. The Canadian Qualen was an actor of wide range, adept at drama and comedy, who had an extensive film career beginning in the early thirties.

A big money-maker for Korda, *Jungle Book* was also recognized with four Oscar nominations - for Cinematography (color), Special Effects, Score and Art Direction (color). That it won none says much for its competition. The winners in those categories that year were *The Black Swan*; *Reap the Wild Wind*; *Now, Voyager*; and *My Gal Sal*, respectively.

Also known as *Rudyard Kipling's Jungle Book* upon

Jungle Book (United Artists, 1942) Poster

its original release, the film received some fine reviews, although there was the usual nitpicking by the less imaginative critics. Sabu was again singled out for his work; Howard Barnes, writing for *The New York Herald Tribune*, was the most lavish in his praise for the actor's performance: "The chief asset of this particular literary classic on the screen, of course, is the presence of Sabu in the role of Mowgli. He is perfect for this motion picture tour de force. Whether he is communing with his friends in the jungle or coping with his enemies in his native village, he gives a direct and unswerving portrayal which holds the production together far more than the script or the spectacular staging." On the other hand, Bosley Crowther of *The New York Times* liked the color and the animals, but felt that "Sabu looks exceedingly silly and most uncomfortable when he has to talk...the film, as a whole, is ostentatious." Ostentatious or not, the original version of *Jungle Book* is highly enjoyable entertainment and a visual banquet.

The animated remake of a generation later from the Disney studio in 1967 is a severely truncated version with the accent on pop music of the period and rather coarse humor, and cannot be compared to the Korda production. Apparently the succeeding hierarchy at Disney realized this, for in 1994, after yet another generation had passed, that studio created a live-action feature version of Kipling's immortal work. Inexplicably, in an era when non-white roles were finally being portrayed on a large scale by actors of the correct ethnicity, the part of Mowgli was given to a young Chinese-American actor named Jason Scott Lee (b. 1966) instead of an Indian actor, although Mowgli as a child was played by an Indian boy. In the credits it is stated that this adaptation is "based on characters created by Rudyard Kipling"; such is the case, as the storyline is really more revisionist Kipling. The British figure prominently in the action and are portrayed as rather a bad lot, except for the girl who falls in love with Mowgli, and her officer father. The well-trained animals retain the Kipling names, but do not speak with human voices as their counterparts did in the 1942 film. Much of the filming was done on location in India, so the art director had less to do than Vincent Korda, although the treasure chamber in the dead city is definitely impressive, as is the city itself. Shere Khan, the tiger, is a catalytic presence throughout this production, and is still alive at the conclusion, another difference from the earlier picture, and from Kipling. Jason Scott Lee does give a credible performance as Mowgli, and the sets, local populace, and music make for an exotic India. It only fails when compared to the imaginative exoticism of Korda's production. One interesting item in this newest version: There is a sturdy and convenient bridge leading to the "forbidden jungle" which all have been told to avoid. Makes one wonder why it was built if no one was allowed to use it.

Seemingly out of nowhere sprang a filmization of Kipling's *The Second Jungle Book* in May of 1997. Produced by Tri-Star Pictures, this version seemed doomed with its unwieldy title: *Rudyard Kipling's 'The Second Jungle Book, Mowgli and Baloo.'* This third remake is strictly pre-teen fare; anyone older will have his or her intelligence insulted. The characters are there - Mowgli, Bagheera, Kaa, Shere Khan, Baloo - but are unrecognizable to lovers of Kipling. The film's cartoonish humor marks it as nothing more than a cheap attempt to cash in on the name of a beloved work of literature. In this misbegotten effort, Mowgli is portrayed by a white boy, and Buldeo has become his uncle. Lawrence Van Gelder of *The New York Times* summed it up very well in his review when he stated: "...and some cobras, which lack the poisonous pizzazz that used to make them such welcome members of the pit bands in the days when film makers like the Korda brothers and George Stevens roamed the Raj in movies like 'Drums' and 'Gunga Din.' Old-fashioned adventure has fallen on hard times." It was no surprise when this travesty was released on video shortly after its brief theatrical run.

On September 29, 1998, the Disney company released yet another version on video only entitled *The Jungle Book - Mowgli's Story*. Obviously made for children, it is nonetheless more faithful to the stories than the Tri-Star film. The animals all have dubbed voices and Mowgli is portrayed by an Indian boy. Near the end, Mowgli discovers a copy of the Kipling book and walks off reading it, hinting that at least one sequel has been planned.

Like many films of the '30s and '40s, *Jungle Book* was dramatized on radio. In the spring of 1942, Sabu crossed the continent to New York, where he appeared on *Rainbow House with Bob Emery*, which broadcast over the Mutual Network. He was introduced as "Sabu, the Elephant Boy" and made a most favorable impression on everyone at the studio, as recalled by Monroe Benton of Brewster, New York, who worked on the show. Sabu even assisted the sound man with the coordination of the jungle sounds.

Sadly, *Jungle Book* was the last film on which all

Jungle Book (United Artists, 1942) Sabu

three Korda brothers collaborated. It is also the last time that Sabu appeared in an Alexander Korda production. The famous producer returned briefly to the scene of his greatest success in September, when he became the first member of the British film industry to be given a knight-hood. Back in Hollywood, Korda laid the groundwork for his permanent return to England when he concluded a deal with Louis B. Mayer of MGM and Loew's Inc. to merge his London Films with MGM's British subsidiary. In May of 1943 he packed his bags and bade farewell to America, returning to Great Britain for good.

Sabu, having fallen in love with the American way of life, and with his brother well settled, chose to remain. An offer of a $1,000 per week contract from Universal Pictures undoubtedly did much to aid his decision, especially since Great Britain was still at war and the young actor was not old enough to enlist. He and Alex Korda parted amicably, for their association had been mutually fruitful. Sabu had been given an exceptional foundation for his career with his first four films. Besides becoming instant classics, they had earned millions of dollars and received a total of seven Academy Award nominations, winning three of those cov-eted trophies for the famed producer. This parting marked the end of the first phase of Sabu's career, the heights of which he would never again attain.

Chapter Eight
The Universal Years

The second phase of Sabu's career began shortly after America's declaration of war against the Axis powers. With the paralyzing attack on Pearl Harbor by Japanese warplanes, the mood of the nation had changed overnight from one of optimism to one of uncertainty. The possibility of an invasion of Hawaii and the mainland had suddenly become very real; mobilization was immediate and intense. Everyone was ready to do his or her bit for the war effort, including, of course, the film industry. Studio executives were well aware how the world situation affected their profits. Having already lost the lucrative European market, they were prepared to do anything to retain the domestic one. As busy as they already were, the studios now became veritable anthills of activity. With gasoline rationed, trips discouraged, and a growing dearth of consumer goods, now more than ever movies were the nation's most popular form of entertainment.

At Universal, meanwhile, Sabu was getting used to the regimen of his new studio. Although now eighteen, he still had to complete his final high-school term, which had been interrupted in 1940 when production on *The Thief of Bagdad* shifted to America, so he attended classes on the lot. As of the beginning of 1942, no property had been found for the former London Films star, so when he was asked by the United States Treasury Department to participate in a War Bond Drive, he eagerly seized the opportunity to show his patriotism. He found that his reputation had preceded him even into the halls of American government; the Department presented him with a baby elephant as a

Sabu and his War Bonds partner

traveling companion. Without stipulating who was to take care of whom, the youthful pair was sent on its merry way across the country with orders to sell, sell, sell War Bonds and Stamps. Beginning the tour in New York in mid-January, Sabu then continued on to Washington, D.C. for further briefing. He visited approximately thirty other cities in the next three months. While he was getting to see the country courtesy of Uncle Sam, brother Dastagir was also contributing his time and sweat working in a defense plant in Los Angeles.

In the early 1930s Universal Pictures made a name for itself with a cycle of well-crafted, highly successful horror pictures. By the middle of the decade, such films were no longer popular with the film-going public, so the studio needed another drawing card to keep afloat. It found one in 1936 when it signed a highly talented young singer who had been let go by MGM. The grosses from Deanna Durbin's films literally saved Universal from bankruptcy. Shortly thereafter, with the acquisition of two former RKO executives, Nate J. Blumberg and Cliff Work, the studio began turning a profit. With the increased production necessitated by the state of war, Universal began churning out pictures in every genre on an assembly-line basis.

It was the idea of producer Walter Wanger (1894-1968) to take a chance on costume adventure pictures. Having been a producer at Paramount, Columbia and MGM, as well as an independent, he already owned a scenario based on *The Arabian Nights* stories which he was anxious to see produced. Arriving at Universal in November 1941, Wanger was granted near-autocratic status. He was given 50% of a film's profits, and was not responsible for losses or budget overruns. After obtaining studio approval at every stage of development, the producer was given "complete supervision and control of the production of the photoplay." Executive Cliff Work was the only person to whom he had to answer. The one concession Wanger was denied was large budgets, though he did go over the imposed limit of $750,000 by $150,000 on his pictures. This, despite the fact that he was only allowed contract players and programmer directors. For *Arabian Nights*, a British freelance writer named Michael Hogan was hired to draft a new version of the fabled tales. Shortly before production began, Wanger also hired True Boardman, who had written an Arabian Nights radio show for Marlene Dietrich, to beef up the story structure and character motivation. Upon reading the Hogan screenplay, Boardman complained that it couldn't be called "Arabian Nights" as it was merely "a western with camels". Wanger said he knew that and was certain it would make a million dollars. Wanger correctly surmised that audiences would like some real escapism from the war headlines and newsreels. The picture grossed almost $3.5 million, yielding $1.9 million in profits.

With an unusual star like Sabu on the company payroll, he had a well-known link to fantasy films readily available. Such a movie would also provide a vehicle for a ravishing young auburn-haired beauty who had been working at the studio for a year in "B" pictures. Maria Montez, the daughter of the Spanish consul to the Dominican Republic, was born there as Maria Africa Vidal Gracia in 1912. She had signed with Universal for $150 per week in 1940. The following year she was seen in several innocuous productions. Although she had leading roles in three of them, only one actually aided her career. In *South of Tahiti* (1941), she wore a sarong for the first time, giving Dorothy Lamour some serious competition. In fact, she was called by some "The Dorothy Lamour of San Fernando Valley", that being the location of the Universal lot. A lady who never had a problem with low self-esteem, Miss Montez continually tooted her own horn in public in an effort to capture attention and thus gain better roles in better pictures. With her gorgeous face and knockout figure, such trumpeting was entirely unnecessary, but it made good copy and eventually got the ambitious actress what she wanted when she was given the female lead in *Arabian Nights*. That she did not betray her fans is evidenced many times in the resulting film, especially in her exhilarating performance in the slave market scene.

Wanger's concept was a lavish tongue-in-cheek adaptation of the world-famous tales of fantasy. He convinced the studio to use Technicolor for the first time since 1930, when they had filmed *The King of Jazz* in the old two-color Technicolor. (Like gasoline, shoes and meat, rationing applied to Technicolor film stock. Production by Technicolor, Inc. was limited to seven million feet per month for the duration.)

Aside from Sabu and Maria Montez, the cast included Jon Hall (1913-1979) as the hero and Leif Erickson (1911-1986) as Hall's overly ambitious brother. Shemp Howard (1900-1955), the sometime Stooge, and John Qualen played Sinbad and Aladdin respectively. The former was continually recalling his past voyages to people who no longer cared, while the latter was forever rubbing lamps in the hopes of retrieving the precious one he had lost. Hal Roach alumnus Billy Gilbert (1893-1971) performs his patented "sneezing" routine, conceived and honed in vaudeville before he entered films, and when dressed in drag has one of his chins tweaked by an amorous soldier. This gives an indication of the level of most of the humor in *Arabian Nights*, which is usually in startling contrast to the occasional brutality of the film. This resulted from the input of Boardman, who had previously worked on Abbott and Costello vehicles.

Also along for the ride in a minor but sinister role was Turhan Bey (b. 1920), who would eventually become Sabu's replacement at the studio. With Sabu, Montez and Bey, Universal had the three most exotic-looking actors this side of Samarkand on its roster of players.

Like *Jungle Book*, the picture is framed by a storyteller, this time a corpulent silver-haired gentleman responsible for the education of a Caliph's harem. He addresses the women in language reminiscent of characters from *The Thief of Bagdad*, calling them "Daughters of foolishness" and "Let us see to the improvement of your minds, what there is of them." He then reads from a copy of *The Arabian Nights* so large that it must be held by two Moorish boys: "Now it happened in Bagdad at this time there was a dancing girl named Scherezade, whose skill and beauty made her the idol of the people. Yet Scherezade, because of the poverty of her childhood, was as avid of power and riches as a shipwrecked mariner of water. Kamar had seen the beauteous maid, and like many another, had fallen madly in love with her."

With the ladies happily engrossed, the storyteller continues: "But Scherezade had spurned his love, saying half in jest and half in earnest, 'Return to me, O Kamar, when you are Caliph of Bagdad and I will listen to you.' But Kamar, besotted by love, had taken the jest in earnest, and rebelling against his brother, had been defeated and captured, thereafter being condemned to suffer the punishment of the Slow Death, even as the law provides."

This scene, which takes place by a small darkened pool on a languid afternoon in the caliph's garden, is one of exquisite beauty, and well shows the seriousness with which Universal approached the film. The camera then delves deep within the pool, and from there pans across a cloud-filled sky to a nightmarish city square at night. There Kamar hangs on a scaffold atop which an impatient vulture sits, while below him an oafish guard dozes. A nearby placard reads: "This is the rebel Kamar al Zaman, who would have destroyed his brother, the great and noble Caliph of Bagdad, Haroun Al-Raschid." The plot of *Arabian Nights* concerns this rivalry between the two brothers for the throne of Bagdad. Kamar's followers rescue him from the scaffold, and attempt to kill Haroun Al-Raschid. He is only wounded, however, and is saved by an acrobat named Ali Ben-Ali (Sabu), who is a member of a poor street circus. This is reminiscent of *The Thief of Bagdad*, as in both films Sabu is surprised that the person he has rescued is a usurped king. Ali hides the ruler's identity from the rest of the troupe of entertainers with whom he travels. Haroun is grudgingly nursed back to health by the tempestuous dancing girl, Scherezade (Montez). The caliph remains with the troupe, biding his time. Meanwhile, Kamar becomes Caliph and seeks Scherezade's hand in marriage. His vizier, Nadan (Edgar Barrier), sees his chance to gain the throne and begins manipulating people to achieve his aim. His final scheme is getting Scherezade to poison Kamar's wine at the wedding. She agrees, but instead intends to take the poison herself. With the cup to her lips, she is stopped by Haroun. His identity exposed, he and his followers battle Kamar and his minions in a rousing finale of burning tents on desert sands. Nadan treacherously kills Kamar during the fight, but is himself slain by one of Ali's troupe. Haroun becomes caliph again and takes Scherezade to be his queen.

Universal, well aware that in order to make money, one must spend it, went all out to make *Arabian Nights* a major box-office hit. Besides using Technicolor and the aforementioned cast, Wanger mustered the studio's best technical talent to make sure that everything went smoothly. This included cinematographer Milton Krasner (1904-1988), who had learned his craft at the old Vitagraph and Biograph studios in New York and went on to become an expert with CinemaScope in the fifties.

Arabian Nights (Universal, 1942)
Billy Gilbert, Sabu, Maria Montez

Location shooting for the desert scenes was done at the sand dunes northwest of Kanab, Utah, and at White Sands National Monument at Alamogordo, New Mexico. The latter locale is the only area of its kind in the world, affording many thousands of acres of natural crystallized gypsum. The footage shot at these sites is the best in the picture at evoking centuries-old Arabia, with mounted figures clad in swirling capes racing across the pristine surfaces of sand and gypsum, their long shadows trailing behind them.

The billowing tent city which appears near the end of the film is memorable as a timeless Arabian mirage among the wind-blown sands of the desert. On a more practical level, it probably saved a good deal of studio set-building time and material, for government restrictions now severely limited the amount of new lumber, paint, and nails that could be used in building motion picture sets. The costumes are as colorful as could be wished, running the gamut from pastels to deeper hues, embellished by precious stones and metals. Equally eye-catching are the background paintings and glass shots, which were executed in vivid tones. However, like the screenplay and the sets, they fail to convey a look or sense of fantasy. Bagdad appears in *Arabian Nights* much like the real city must have looked, not at all like the otherworldly cosmopolis of *The Thief of Bagdad*. Of course, it may have been Wanger's intention to focus attention on the players by not overwhelming them with the sets, or possibly the studio ordered him to keep costs down. Whatever the case, the fantasy touch is non-existent, as noted by critic Bosley Crowther, who described the film in *The New York Times* as "... just a lush Technicolored romance, completely devoid of fantasy..." Considering that fantasy is the strongest element of *The Arabian Nights* tales, it is surprising none surfaced in this film. Its story is as real as history. Only once does fantasy intrude, when Sabu produces a wine cup seemingly from nowhere and then throws it in the air, where it vanishes. No explanation for this magic feat is given.

On the plus side is Frank Skinner's (1897-1968) stirring score, appropriately up-tempo during the action scenes and suitably seductive for the romantic interludes. For Scherezade's wedding dance, he adds a clever touch with a variation on a theme from the "Arabian Dance" from Tchaikovsky's *The Nutcracker* ballet. This dance is so erotically seductive it is a minor miracle that the censors of the day gave it clearance.

Sabu entered into the fun with his usual élan, making a spectacular entrance with a series of handsprings. He must have realized, though, that his career had taken a dip artistically, if not financially. As in *The Thief of Bagdad*, his is the most nimble brain among the leads, and he is involved in much of the skullduggery and the action, which includes leading a charge of mounted soldiers during the film's climactic battle.

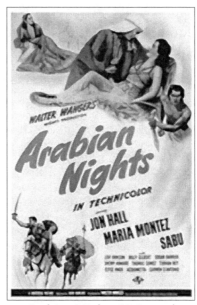

Arabian Nights (Universal, 1942) Poster

One bit of fun occurs when Sabu seeks to enter the harem for the purpose of delivering a message to Scherezade. The guard informs Sabu that it is forbidden for any man but the Caliph and the Lord Vizier to enter. Sabu innocently replies: "But I'm not a man - I'm only a boy." "Boys grow fast," states the guard in a bit of timeless wisdom which seems to have caught the Hays Office asleep. (An earlier draft of the script had the guard saying: "Boys grow fast around here.")

Sabu's popularity with the public and critics continued,

The Hollywood Reporter declaring, "...Sabu actively engaging as the clever Arab waif who sparks the rescue of his ruler and makes Scherezade's dream of being queen come true." *Variety's* reviewer seemed quite impressed by the production, stating: "...script and direction keep things moving at a consistently fast clip, with dialogue crisp throughout"; "Hall delivers a satisfactory and heroic performance in lead, with Sabu also neatly spotted"; "Miss Montez catches audience attention as the alluring and eyeful dancing girl. Performance will lift her several notches in popularity, with indications Universal has a glamour girl on its list for future assignments."

Miss Montez, despite an accent as thick as Bela Lugosi's, survived that handicap and found herself with a larger following than ever, as *Variety's* critic had predicted. She was apparently comfortable working with director John Rawlins (1902-1997), who had already directed her in *Raiders of the Desert* (1941) and *Bombay Clipper* (1942). He would direct her once more, in the 1945 release *Sudan*.

Jon Hall, the Fresno boy who grew up on Tahiti, seemed to have found his niche, for most of his subsequent films involved either costumed adventure or an island setting. The son of an ice-skating champion and a Tahitian woman, Jon made the move to television in the early fifties, starring in the popular adventure series *Ramar of the Jungle*, while continuing to appear in films. He developed a special underwater camera for the Navy and rented out other cameras he owned to the studios. He was married to singer Frances Langford (1914-2005) and to Mexican actress Raquel Torres (1908-1987). In December 1979, after being told that he had an inoperable cancer, the sixty-six-year-old former star took his own life. Fans may remember him best as the lithe native hero in John Ford's *The Hurricane* (1937), although he did tend to bulk up in later years.

As previously mentioned, Turhan Bey later replaced Sabu at Universal; proving equally difficult to cast due to the extreme exoticism of his features, he faded from the film scene in the early fifties. Photography being his first love, he returned to Vienna, the city of his birth, and set up shop as a photographer. Although his business thrived, he now lives in Los Angeles, having, in the 1990s, revived his show-business career by appearing on several popular American television series, such as *SeaQuest* and *Murder, She Wrote* and in a couple of minor feature films.

The studio's investment in *Arabian Nights* paid off handsomely; besides the film's impressive gross, it garnered four Academy Award nominations: Cinematography (color), Art Direction/Interior Decoration (color), Sound Recording, and Scoring of a Dramatic/Comedy film. Unfortunately, it did not win in any of these categories. On a lesser note, the picture was chosen by *Life* magazine for its "Movie of the Week" feature and began a cycle of what the Hollywood hierarchy fondly referred to as "sand and sarong" movies.

These facts, coupled with the emergence of Maria Montez and Jon Hall as an exciting new romantic team, convinced the studio to produce a follow-up feature with the same star trio.

From an original story by Peter Milne sprang a screenplay from future director Richard Brooks (1912-1992) called *White Savage*. It is a simple tale of love and greed on a South Pacific isle. Evil white men lust greedily after the priceless gems and gold in a sacred pool on peaceful Temple Island, which is ruled by the beauteous (and available) Princess Tahia (Montez). Handsome, muscular (and single) fisherman Kaloe (Hall) seeks the right to hunt sharks near the island for the Vitamin A found in their livers. The evil white men corrupt Tahia's younger brother, Tamara (Turhan Bey), by teaching him how to gamble and drink. While Kaloe romances Tahia, Tamara continues to lose at cards, until he is driven to putting up the deed to Temple Island once he is out of cash. Kaloe sits in on the game, however, and manages to win the pot containing the deed, while keeping Miller, the head baddie, from cheating. Tamara, in his cups, punches Kaloe and stalks out. Miller later brings Tamara's body to Tahia, with Kaloe's knife in its back. With some help from a local jack-of-all-trades named Wong, Kaloe gets the real killer to sign a confession, implicating Miller.

The time for subtlety past, Miller and his cohorts take a motor boat to Temple Island and proceed to dynamite the sacred pool, allowing the water to flow out so that they can obtain the gold and gems. This action angers the local god, Tangaroa, who, with the help of the special effects crew,

White Savage (Universal, 1943) Title card

causes an earthquake that destroys most of the island's structures, some of which conveniently fall upon Miller and his minions. Hero wins Princess, and everyone is happy again, completely overlooking the damage estimates and the clean-up.

Director Arthur Lubin (1901-1995) handled this unpretentious exercise in exotica with his usual workmanlike precision. Aside from Universal's lavish remake of *The Phantom of the Opera* (1943), Lubin was more at home with the likes of Abbott and Costello comedies and, later, Francis the Talking Mule. He did direct *Ali Baba and the Forty Thieves* (1944) with Montez and Hall, though, as well as the 1961 remake of *The Thief of Bagdad*. Still, he was a capable gentleman and should be more remembered.

Sabu played Hall's young native friend and experienced another decline in his fortunes; he began speaking Pidgin English. To wit: "Sorry for self no good." and "How you know Tahia like that?" This, after three years in an exclu-

sive English board-
ing school! He was
not given much to
do in this picture ex-
cept look handsome
and be a mischie-
vous matchmaker
between Kaloe and
Tahia. He was pretty
much a "sidekick",

White Savage (Universal, 1943)
Sabu, Jon Hall

although kids in the audience could surely identify with
him. Tarzan had "Boy", Red Ryder had "Little Beaver",
someone to pal around with and maybe go fishing with
when nobody needed heading off at the pass. Sabu, in
these distant and fantasied realms, fitted these rules perfectly. He came with the territory. Sabu does rescue Kaloe
from a small arena occupied by several lionesses. (Only
God and the prop man know where lions are to be found
on a South Pacific island.) Miss Montez is as lovely and
haughty as ever, though still in need of elocution lessons,
and Jon Hall looks tanner, trimmer, and somewhat more
relaxed than in his other pictures.

Thomas Gomez (1905-1971) and Paul Guilfoyle (1902-
1961) lent their considerable talents in the roles of the
chief do-badders, and Sidney Toler (1874-1947), the then-
current Charlie Chan, furnished better comic relief than

Sabu did as a man of many hats with an astute business sense and a soft heart. A dance sequence seemingly choreographed by a bush Busby Berkeley involving giant drums provided an interesting but brief interlude from the fast-moving plot. Location shooting included Dana Point and the beach at Balboa, California. *White Savage* took but thirty-six days to film, as opposed to forty-eight for *Arabian Nights*. Most critics lauded the Technicolor photography, but had little use for any of the film's other elements, as shown by Theodore Strauss' review in *The New York Times*: "For our part Universal may keep the deed to Temple Island." According to Jay Robert Nash and Stanley Ralph Ross in their *Motion Picture Guide* (Cinebooks, Chicago, 1987), "*White Savage* is the quintessential second-rate adventure film. It features a ludicrous plot, silly dialog, lurid Technicolor, attractive women in sarongs, and two leads who together couldn't act their way out of a paperbag, but who look good." Continuing: "However, it was exactly what wartime audiences wanted to see, lightweight entertainment that had nothing to do with reality."

At the end of 1943 Sabu was seen in his first short, one of Columbia's long-running series known as *Screen Snapshots*. His footage consisted of his playing volleyball, arranging seats for an outdoor theater, dumping garbage, and removing his shoes and socks; rather like going from the sublime to the ridiculous. He did not interact with any of the other celebrities, who include among others, Jimmy Durante, George Jessel, Gig Young, the Ritz Brothers, and Bronco Billy Anderson. Maybe it is just as well that he did not.

With money still rolling in from *White Savage*, Universal wasted no time developing another vehicle for La Montez, who was now known as "The Queen of Technicolor". *Ali Baba and the Forty Thieves* was the new project, and Sabu was slated to be Montez's bodyguard and friend. But as he had enlisted in the army in the meantime, he was replaced by Turhan Bey. Almost as lavishly produced as *Arabian Nights*, *Ali Baba* paid off even better, prompting Universal to keep Maria Montez hopping from one picture to another.

After a cameo appearance in the studio's all-star variety feature *Follow The Boys* (1944), it was back to scantier costumes and a reunion with Sabu and Jon Hall for *Cobra Woman*, surely the "camp champ" of the '40s. Imagine Maria as twins, one good, one evil, the latter high priestess of a snake cult who periodically dances before a live king cobra prior to ordering numerous worshipers to their deaths in a volcano. Considering that she wants more revenue, killing perfectly good taxpayers seems an odd way to obtain it. Imagine also that all this takes place on a tropical island where no intruder who sets foot ever returns. Yet copies of *Vogue* magazine somehow get through, as all the island's female hierarchy is dressed in the latest 1944 fashions. Throw in a standard, irritating Hollywood chimpanzee and a Sabu sleepwalking scene that need give no Lady Macbeth any cause for concern, and you get some idea of the shenanigans that abound in this glorious potboiler.

Though given the same general setting as *White Savage*, the South Seas, *Cobra Woman* features a larger cast and more action. The use of Technicolor is again a definite plus, especially in showing Maria's shimmering cobra costume. Not all of the sets were built especially for this production, however; any movie purist will recognize much he had already seen, such as the dungeon from *Tower of London* (1939) and the pagan altar from *Green Hell* (1940).

Sabu received a special medical discharge from the Army to appear in *Cobra Woman*. It is a wonder that he did not need one afterwards. Again, he ran around bare-chested and bare-legged, speaking Pidgin English: "I are best man" and "Big fellow stranger, no eyes, no tongue." This time there was no excuse for his language, as his character was attending a missionary school. Of course, considering the "happy-go-lucky" character he was again portraying, he could have been failing English or had an inept instructor. Then again, everyone on Cobra Island, except for those in power, speaks just as poorly; most of the dialogue makes the guttural mutterings of Johnny Weissmuller's Tarzan sound Shakespearean by comparison.

The reviewer for *The Hollywood Reporter* summed up Sabu's work by stating "[Sabu] is excellent in this appearance and purveys quite a bit of incidental comedy with a well-trained chimpanzee." One thing is certain: the Sabu character is not impressed by titles. Upon meeting the queen of Cobra Island, he shakes her hand and says, "Pleased to meet you!"

Maria Montez is at her most sinuous, slithering and wriggling about in her form-hugging outfits as only she knew how. The cobra headdress she wears as high priestess rivals anything ever devised for Carmen Miranda. Much has been made of her portraying the disparate sisters with a singular lack of distinction between them; but after all, her name was Montez, not Duse. But this did make it difficult for an unusually dense Jon Hall to tell them apart in the film. Maria was cast in costume films for her beauty and sex appeal, not her histrionic ability, and on that level she succeeded very well. The critics had a field day trying to out-do each other in attacking this comedy of errors. Bosley Crowther of *The New York Times* put it best when he wrote (under the heading "Snakebite Remedy"): "That beautiful land of nowhere which Universal has carved out of the blue for the recently recurring caprices of Maria Montez, Jon Hall and Sabu again rocks to exotic music... and again the submissive audience is witchingly rocked to sleep with as wacky an adventure fable as was ever dished up outside the comic strips." He added, "The Dance of the King Cobra is howlingly honky-tonk...." and later: "It is better than the funny papers on which it is obviously based." Archer Winston of *The New York Post* called *Cobra*

Woman "...Tarzan of the Pacific, Shangri-La with water, Bagdad by the beach plus a volcano." Said Alton Cook of *The New York World-Telegram*: "The main idea of the picture is to have Maria Montez scampering around in thin dresses, Technicolor

Cobra Woman (Universal, 1944) Lon Chaney, Sabu, Lois Collier

and no underwear." Not content with that, the critic went on: "Lon Chaney is in the picture as a mute...He may have had an argument with the writer on the idiotic dialogue provided for him, so a compromise was made." As in *White Savage*, Jon Hall went through the required motions of portraying the all-American klutz. In his way he was as stylized as the Montez character, though lacking the heavy accent.

When Ramu's (Hall) fiancée Tollea (Montez) is kidnapped and taken to Cobra Island on the pair's wedding day, Ramu trails her there, even though he knows that death is meted out to all intruders. His young friend Kado (Sabu) stows away on his boat and together they seek Tollea. Ramu finds Nadja, her evil twin, instead, in a beautifully-executed jungle swimming scene. He mistakes Nadja for his fiancée and reacts accordingly. He is caught and imprisoned, but later escapes. Kado, meanwhile, locates Tollea. Together they witness the Dance of the King Cobra from a vantage point in the temple, thereby showing the audience how the ritual ordinarily proceeded. Ramu is taken to the queen, who explains the origin of the twins. Tollea, as firstborn, is the rightful ruler of Cobra Island. When the girls were but a year old, they were subjected to cobra bites; Tollea fainted, Nadja did not; Tollea was taken away and Nadja later became ruler. Now Nadja's cruelty and heavy taxation have become too much to bear, so the queen had Tollea brought back to the island to supplant Nadja. She urges Ramu to leave Cobra Island without Tollea. Ramu tries to leave with Kado, but they are caught by Nadja's guards. In the meantime, Martok, Nadja's cohort, kills the interfering queen, and Tollea confronts Nadja. Nadja tries to kill her sister, but stumbles out a window to her death. Ramu and Kado are already in the temple awaiting death, but Tollea, impersonating Nadja, halts the execution. Smelling a rat (or reading about the substitution in the script) Martok orders the cobra ritual to proceed. In a sequence of growing excitement Tollea attempts the deadly dance, but faints just as the cobra strikes. Kado, his bonds cut by his ever-faithful chimp, kills the snake with his poison dart gun. They begin fighting their way out just as the volcano erupts and everyone panics. Martok is killed in the ensuing confusion and the volcano, as if on cue, becomes silent. Ramu and Kado then head for home on their boat and are surprised to find that Tollea has stowed away to be with Ramu. It was only natural and fitting that in those pre-feminist days Tollea would give up being queen of a tropical island in order to serve her husband-to-be.

Interestingly enough, an earlier draft of *Cobra Woman* had the island sinking into the sea just after the main characters escaped. This concept was wisely abandoned as the only two evil people on the island had been killed, and it was no longer sufficiently wicked to be destroyed.

Production values are above average for this type of picture; Vera West's costumes exhibit an imaginative flair and the set decorations serve the cobra motif well. Especially impressive is the cobra throne in the temple, a monstrous version of the real thing, made of solid gold, fangs bared and tongue protruding. Edward Ward's (1900-1971) score is appropriate in its heavy use of percussion instruments for the temple scenes and its reliance on strings for the quieter moments. (Ward had earlier composed a tango entitled "Song of Midnight", which was reportedly inspired by La Montez. When he played a recording of it for Maria, she was so delighted to hear it played by a full orchestra instead of the expected piano solo that she broke down in tears.)

The color photography for *Cobra Woman* is luminous, accentuating the lushness of the efflorescent verdure and the radiance of the tropical sun. Both *The Hollywood Reporter* and *Variety* gave high marks to the camera work, the former stating: "...Technicolored splendors...are neatly managed by the cameras of George Robinson and W. Howard Greene," while the latter raved: "Photography... is of high standard."

Cobra Woman (Universal, 1944) Poster

Some fans may be surprised to learn that *Cobra Woman* was directed by Robert Siodmak, a master of film noir. Though he was born in the U.S. in 1900, he grew up in Germany where he began his film career. He returned to the States after fleeing the Nazi regime. Occasionally collaborating with his screenwriter brother Curt (1902-2000), Siodmak was responsible for such classics as *The Spiral Staircase* (1945) and *The Killers* (1946). He died in 1973.

Despite, or perhaps because of, the humorous goings-on, *Cobra Woman* proved to be another bonanza for Universal. Montez' career continued apace, but it would be two years before Sabu again set foot upon a soundstage. However, it was around this time that the formation of a national fan club for Sabu was announced in *Movie Star*

Parade magazine, a sign that his popularity continued to grow. His work on the picture completed, he rushed back to Harlingen Army Air Base and within a few months was on his way to more distant islands in the South Pacific. (See Chapter 9).

Productions such as *Cobra Woman* and *White Savage*, while seriously lacking in profundity, nevertheless performed a service by giving Americans some breathing space after they had heard the latest news from actual Pacific islands with names like Corregidor and Bataan. Although these movies had their share of violent scenes, they were nothing compared to those occurring at thousands of places all over the globe at the time, nor were they as real.

With his military service behind him, Sabu returned to a new Hollywood. The war had greatly affected the tastes of filmgoers, as it had everything else. Stark realism, the new film noir style, proved to be the biggest box-office draw. While stories of exotica and fantasy were still being made, they were few and far between and did not fare so well in terms of ticket sales. Into this changed environment came Sabu, wiser but no sadder for his war experience, ready for whatever lay ahead.

His return to the studio was a personal triumph, as everyone from stars to prop men gathered around to shake his hand and pound him on the back before hoisting him in the air in tribute to his wartime heroics.

The actor's return to filmmaking was less than auspicious, however, considering that fine and well-publicized service record. Though he still owed Universal one film, they had nothing prepared for him. Rather than spend the time selecting a scenario suitable for Sabu's image, the studio rushed him into a project already in production, a spy thriller entitled *Tangier*. Screenwriters M.M. Musselman and Monty F. Collins were ordered to create a character for Sabu so that he could finish his contract. Apparently, the studio heads had already realized that there would be no place for an "elephant boy" in their future productions. Unfortunately for the ex-gunner, his part in *Tangier* really looks like a last-minute addition.

As Pepe, a young man who sings for patrons of a hotel restaurant and is willing to perform other services, Sabu does get to sing three songs, speaks normal English for the first time since *Arabian Nights*, and is completely clothed in either a shirt and slacks or a suit and tie. While his outer image was altered, he was still the hero's friend and treated like a boy. Although given third billing, he disappears for long stretches and does not figure in any of the action scenes. Were it not for the songs, his role would have been entirely overlooked. As it was, almost every reviewer mentioned his crooning rendition of "She'll Be Comin' Round the Mountain" as one of the film's highlights. (There is no record of Bing Crosby's reaction.) The voice had matured along with the man, showing promise had Sabu cared to hone that particular talent.

The story takes place in early summer 1945. The Hitlerian war is over. Nazis are fleeing Allied wrath in all corners of the globe, changing identities or committing suicide. Among the former is one who is responsible for the deaths of many innocents; he is in Tangier to obtain a diamond with which to finance his identity change. Both a Spanish dancer and a discredited American journalist are seeking him; the former to avenge the deaths of her brothers and father, the latter to report on the Nazi, thereby restoring his standing in the fourth estate. Their paths cross and they fall in love, but not before several complications occur, culminating in the Nazi's death and the recovery of the diamond.

For this black-and-white *Casablanca* pastiche, Sabu was reunited with Maria Montez for their fourth and final film together. Playing the male lead this time was Robert Paige (1910-1987) instead of Jon Hall. Paige had been kicking around mostly in "B" pictures at the studio for some time and was apparently grateful for a change of pace. He does a creditable job in his role of the journalist, his less than heroic looks and physique being just right for such a character. Miss Montez was as gorgeous as ever, perhaps more so as she was carrying her first child, a fact which required both creative direction and costuming. (She had married French actor Jean-Pierre Aumont on July 13, 1943). She even seemed to have learned a bit about dramatics, handling some of her scenes very well, especially the one in which the journalist reminisces about his days in Madrid, causing her to do likewise. As she recalls her childhood and adolescence, including the horrors of the Spanish Civil War, Maria actually seems to be remembering some painful experience.

Capably filling the supporting roles were such experienced players as Preston Foster, Kent Taylor, Louise Allbritton, and the imposingly-named J. Edward Bromberg. The 6'2" Foster (1900-1970) had been playing both heroes and heavies since 1930. With his commanding voice, he brought the necessary swaggering presence to his role as the military governor. Kent Taylor (1906-1987) was likewise a veteran leading man, but much more the suave, sophisticated type than Foster. As Ramon, Rita's (Montez') dancing partner, he added a certain touch of class to the proceedings. Svelte blonde Louise Allbritton (1920-1979) came in second to Maria Montez in every department - glamour, love, and billing. Maria got the better costumes (striking creations by Travis Banton), won the leading man, and was, of course, the star. Louise had to content herself with being Rita's dance double and losing both the object of her affections and her life in the last reel. Hungarian-born J. Edward Bromberg's (1903-1951) stocky figure was a familiar one to film fans by the time he appeared in *Tangier*. In this film he replaced Peter Lorre, who was the original choice for the role of the head of an organization concerned with the recovery of Nazi treasure.

Production values are high, with a very handsome hotel set the centerpiece for most of the action. Woody Bredell's (1884-1976) film-noirish cinematography gives the picture a nice sheen and the costumes aside from Maria's are equally attractive. Reviews were

Universal publicity shot, 1945

generally mediocre, as exemplified by that in *Variety:* "*Tangier* is spy melodrama with plenty of hokum. It's not a good example of dialoging or directing, but thrill ingredients make it acceptable. Maria Montez and Robert Paige, particularly the latter, spark the lead roles as much as possible. Sabu, as a native guide...supplies some chuckles and the vocal moments on 'She'll Be Comin' 'Round the Mountain', 'Polly Wolly Doodle', and 'Love Me Tonight'". A.H. Weiler, writing in *The New York Times*, had this to say: "*Tangier*...gets scant help from either its setting or its star. ... Miss Montez' array of clothes is far more impressive than the picture's plot and the people involved in it."

Released in March of 1946, the unfortunate failure of

Tangier at the box office sounded a death knell for the career of Maria Montez at Universal. *The Motion Picture Guide* pretty well sums up the film by stating: "Set in Tangier, Africa, it should have stayed there." Surely her many fans demanded and deserved Technicolor, and were not so ready to accept her in anything less. Though only the first of her films to lose money, that was enough for the dollar-conscious men who ran the studio, which was soon to merge with International Pictures, becoming Universal-International. She made only two more pictures for them, *The Exile* and *Pirates of Monterey* (both 1947) and one for United Artists, *Siren of Atlantis* (1949), before departing for Europe and her final four films. Her untimely demise at the age of thirty-nine, in 1951, from a heart seizure suffered while taking a very hot saline bath, deprived the film world of one of its more colorful personalities. Her type of role does not fit well in the harsh world of today.

Also in March, Sabu appeared in *Screen Snapshots* again. This time all he does is take a cameo bow along with some other stars, as Alan Mowbray got the lion's share of the action in this nine-and-a-half-minute filler.

Sabu, as previously mentioned, was already considered passé by the Universal hierarchy and was not offered a new contract. (To be fair to Universal, it must be mentioned that they had paid all their employees who had served in the armed forces during the war 25% of their salaries for their period of service.) While at 22 he was not ready to give up acting, Sabu must have had second thoughts about continuing his film career. He had never been without a contract. Freelancing was a new situation for him, yet he would give it the old Beaconstone try. Thus ended the second phase of Sabu's film career, a rewarding one financially, but not artistically. His days with the brothers Korda and their timeless, handcrafted films, now lay in the distant past. It was a new post-war period, and the future was unknown.

Chapter Nine
Uncle Sam Calls

After several disastrous setbacks in the Pacific theater of the war in the first few months of 1942, the U.S. armed forces had their initial success at the Battle of the Coral Sea in May, followed by a major naval victory at the Battle of Midway in June. In the latter engagement, the Japanese fleet suffered so heavily that Japan's formerly superior naval strength was reduced to one of equality with the Allies. Guadalcanal Island was the first land conquest for the Americans, who invaded there in August of 1942. Japanese forces finally evacuated the island in January-February of 1943 and began fighting defensively. Nevertheless, their navy continued to take a toll on Allied shipping.

Such was the situation in the Far East when Sabu enlisted in the U.S. Army in July of 1943, with the intention of becoming an aviation cadet. His request was denied because he was not an American citizen. Initially assigned to a ground crew and stationed at Santa Ana Army Air Base in

California, he was transferred to Fort Meade in Maryland, where he continued his basic training. It was during his seven months there that he received a special deferment enabling him to appear in *Cobra Woman* for Universal back in Hollywood. It was also during this period that a memorable moment occurred for the young Indian. On January 4, 1944, the one-time stable boy from Mysore, Selar Shaik, now internationally famous as "Sabu, the Elephant Boy", became a citizen of the United States; a prouder and more loyal American would have been extremely difficult to find.

When the Universal star participated in "The Music Hall Revue" in a segment entitled "Hollywood at Ft. Meade" and hosted a weekly radio program for GI's called "Your Army Quiz Show", it appeared that he still would not get his wish to see aerial action. These show-business activities resulted in his being asked by the Special Service Office of the Army Ground Forces to remain at Ft. Meade as an entertainer. Determined to see action, the new U.S. citizen requested a transfer to the Army Air Corps. In his letter to his commanding officer, Sabu stated that due to his interest in and knowledge of mechanics, he could better serve his country in that capacity. This request was granted, and he was again transferred, this time to Greensboro, North Carolina, for basic training in aerial gunnery. Continuing that training at the Harlingen, Texas, Army Air Field, Sabu won his "gunner's wings" after an intensive seven-week course, emerging as a private first class.

While he was stationed there, the premiere of *Cobra Woman* was held in Atlantic City, New Jersey on April 25. A forty-five-minute musical revue bearing the same title as the film was put together at Harlingen and broadcast over radio station KGBS. The same station also aired a brief outline of Sabu's career on a program called *G.I. Jubilee*. By the mid-summer of 1944, the twenty-year-old celebrity had become a member of the 307th Bombardment Group of the 13th Army Air Force and found himself en route to the South Pacific as a gunner on a B-24 Liberator. He could have used his pull as a movie star in order to avoid any dangerous involvement in the war effort; instead, he chose extremely hazardous duty, proving his patriotism beyond question. His outfit, known as "The Long Rangers" because their planes were capable of sustained missions, was based on New Guinea. Their area of operations included the entire southwest sector of the Pacific Ocean, from Australia to Leyte to Borneo. Once, over the last-named locale, Sabu's plane single-handedly attacked a five-ship Japanese convoy. Flying determinedly through heavy anti-aircraft fire, the B-24's crew sank a transport and a freighter, damaged two cargo ships, and had a near miss on the fifth vessel. For this heroic encounter, every member of the crew was awarded the Distinguished Flying Cross. Sabu's luck followed him into the service; due to his small frame of 5'4" and 125 pounds, he was able to take a parachute with him into his cramped quarters.

Had his plane ever been seriously hit he could have "hit the silk", but it never was, although the crew had its share of close calls.

Given leave in January 1945, Sabu went to Sydney, Australia, where he called on his friend

Sabu at his surprise birthday party in Sydney, January 1945 - Photo courtesy of Mitchell Library, State Library of New South Wales, Sydney, Australia

Bob Dyer, who was the star of a radio show there. Dyer was a British comedian whom Sabu had met in London while filming *The Thief of Bagdad*. Invited by the radio personality to appear on his program, the motion picture celebrity was pleasantly surprised when the audience rose and sang "Happy Birthday" to him in tribute to his attaining the age of twenty-one.

In July of that year, Allied forces took the city of Balikpapan on Borneo, thereby cutting off a major source of oil for the Japanese Army. Sabu and his buddies saw action in the air over Balikpapan, which turned out to be the actor's final engagement of the war. Before the month was over, the film star, who was called both "Sab" and "Junior" by his crew mates, was back in Hollywood with the rank of staff sergeant. He had flown 42 missions totaling 425 hours in the air. For his gallant service, besides the DFC he had earned for the action over Borneo, Sabu was awarded the Air Medal with three oak leaf clusters, four battle stars on the Asiatic-Pacific campaign medal, a Presidential Unit Citation, the Victory Medal, and the good conduct medal. His superiors wrote many letters commending Sabu's character, patriotism, and integrity. Only on a thirty-day furlough, but with enough points for discharge, the new American citizen was ready to continue defending his country by returning to frontline action. That gesture proved unnecessary when Japan surrendered on August 14, ending the most destructive war yet witnessed by mankind. Even that momentous event did not stop the young actor from serving his country; for a period after the war, he was a second lieutenant in the Civil Air Patrol. As for millions of other returning soldiers, Sabu found the problems of a post-war world looming before him.

Chapter Ten
Two for the Archers

Free of contractual obligations after wrapping up his meager work on *Tangier*, Sabu was at liberty to accept any enticing offers which might come his way. Receiving one from his old friend Michael Powell, he crossed the Atlantic Ocean to Great Britain for his first visit there after six busy and exciting years in the United States.

Since his work on *The Thief of Bagdad*, Powell had directed a number of outstanding films, among them *49th Parallel* (1941), *The Life and Death of Colonel Blimp* (1943) and *A Matter of Life and Death* (1946). Made in collaboration with Emeric Pressburger, the Hungarian writer to whom Alex Korda had introduced him at a script conference for *The Spy in Black*, these productions had catapulted the pair into the front ranks of British filmmakers. In 1942 they had formed their own outfit, The Archers, and had become members of the original board of Production Managers of Independent Producers, a group formed by

J. Arthur Rank to handle business and legal aspects of production within his organization, which included Gaumont-British and the Odeon chain of theaters. The Archers created a unique cinematic logo for themselves: a target in which several arrows were scattered about in the outer circles, then one final arrow whizzing into the bull's-eye just before the credits began. Rank (1888-1972) allowed The Archers a choice of studios between Denham, Alex Korda's former base of operations, and the newer Pinewood. They opted for the latter for its better layout, which facilitated travel and communication among the various departments.

All of their productions through 1946 had been original ideas of the team; Pressburger had even won an Oscar for Best Screenplay for *49th Parallel*. Their current project, *Black Narcissus*, was based on a novel by an authoress named Rumer Godden. The highly unusual book had been suggested to Powell as potential film material by actress Mary Morris during the war, and again by Emeric Pressburger after it. Upon reading the novel, Powell was firmly convinced of its filmic possibilities.

With a mainly Indian setting, *Black Narcissus* tells the story of an order of Anglican nuns based in Calcutta who are invited by the ruler of a remote state in the Himalayas to set up a community to serve the educational and medical needs of the local populace. He gives them a windy palace perilously perched atop a cliff in which a former rajah had kept his concubines. In keeping with local tradition, it has long been known as "The House of Women".

Complicating things is the local British agent, a lanky privacy-loving English eccentric named Dean, whose earthy good looks awaken the latent sexuality of Sister Ruth, one of the new young nuns. In time the extreme isolation and primal mysticism of this forgotten portion of the world unhinge Ruth's mind, and in a final act of desperation, she deserts the order. Wearing bright red lipstick and a matching mail-order dress, she descends the unworldly ramparts of the still half-pagan palace to the lush tropical valley where Dean resides in semi-barbaric comfort. He spurns her advances, which unbalances her further, and she reclimbs the treacherous steps and in a scene of wild abandon, attempts to push the Sister Superior off the cliff. Instead, she loses her own footing and falls to the depths below. This proves to be the final travail suffered by the nuns, and they leave the mountain top, never to return. The crumbling palace and its richness of erotic friezes are reclaimed by the winds and the hedonistic forces of antiquity.

Sabu was probably the easiest to cast in this perplexing tale; he was given the part of the son of the ruler of the Indian kingdom. He was honored to be selected to play the character who gives the story its title, *Black Narcissus*, that being a cologne worn by the youth. He also got to wear finery surpassing that which he wore in the final scene of *The Thief of Bagdad*. Powell, who always did his own casting, knew that there was no one else suitable to portray Dilip Rai, the young general, and was thrilled when Sabu accepted the role so readily. As he stated in his autobiography, "The young General in Rumer Godden's book, and our script, was an attractive character. He was a boy with all a boy's charm and innocence, but with the power of life and death. He speaks English well but uses it in his own way...He is friendly and eager, but he also has charm and authority...it was a part tailor-made for Sabu, who possessed all these qualities." (Author Rumer Godden reportedly did not applaud Powell's selection of Sabu. She thought the Indian actor totally unsuitable, referring to him as "a thick-set, snout-nosed South Indian coolie boy." Upon seeing the finished film, she was even more incensed, calling it "...an absolute travesty of the book" and "...an abomination.")

The director literally burned the telegraph wires dickering with famed Shakespearean actor/director Laurence Olivier over the services of a daintily beautiful teenager from London named Jean Simmons (1929-2010). He wanted her for Kanchi, the Indian dancing girl who runs off with Dilip Rai, while Olivier wanted her for Ophelia in his production of *Hamlet*. Since they were both filming at the same studio, an amicable solution was reached whereby the adolescent actress divided her time between the two productions, giving memorable performances in both films, further proof of why there will always be an England.

After being convinced by Deborah Kerr (1921-2007) that she could play a woman ten years her senior, Powell had to bargain with Ben Goetz, the head of MGM's British operation, in order to get her. MGM owned half of her contract, but presently had no work for her. (After seeing her strong performance in *Black Narcissus*, they bought the other half and the red-headed actress went on to a long and illustrious career in Hollywood.) The two finally settled on a figure, and Kerr had the role of Sister Clodagh, who heads the mission at Saint Faith, as the order had dubbed the Himalayan palace.

For the Englishman, Mr. Dean, The Archers settled on David Farrar (1908-1995), whose screen test so impressed them that they put him under contract for three films. A journalist-turned-actor with a saturnine countenance, Farrar had been appearing in films for a decade without setting the world on fire.

The plum role of Sister Ruth, whose libido is stirred by Dean, and whose differences with Sister Clodagh create the central conflict in the picture, went to Kathleen Byron, (1922-2009), a twenty-four-year-old actress who had played an angel in *A Matter of Life and Death*. Powell chose her for her unusual looks - long, pointed nose, high cheekbones and big eyes. (Her memorable performance inspired a British television documentary made in 1997 by

Malcolm Venville called "Remembering Sister Ruth".) For the other nuns, the director picked actresses of proven ability, most notably Flora Robson (1902-1984), the highly esteemed stage actress whose previous film appearances had included a pair of portrayals of Queen Elizabeth I - *Fire Over England* (1936) and *The Sea Hawk* (1940). She was to play Sister Philippa, a nun with a gift for gardening. The physically imposing Judith Furse (1912-1974) was to be Sister Briony, a no-nonsense woman able to take charge in any situation, and Scottish Jenny Laird (1917-2001) would have the part of Sister Blanche, popularly called "Sister Honey", whose heart went out to everyone, but most of all to children.

To portray the aged housekeeper, a holdover from The House of Women, who stays on to aid the nuns, Powell selected May Hallatt (1876-1969), a septuagenarian stage actress noted for her character roles. With her rasping voice and nervous mannerisms, she stole every scene in which she appeared. ("What do they eat? How do I know what nuns eat?")

When the first script conference for *Black Narcissus* was held, the director had answers ready for every question thrown at him. The exteriors would all be shot in a garden in Horsham, Sussex, known for its sub-tropical flora. This tactic kept costs down and allowed Production Designer Alfred Junge (1886-1964) an opportunity to create some truly impressive sets, especially the palace the nuns attempt to convert into a combination clinic/school. For that elaborate structure Junge and his crew erected a full-size building at Pinewood that allowed cnematographer Jack Cardiff and his assistants to move freely from room to room with their equipment. Junge had been a designer for the Berlin State Opera and State Theater before

Black Narcissus (Archer Prod./General Film, 1947) Poster

becoming an Art Director at Ufa, Germany's pre-eminent film studio, in 1920. He settled in Britain in the early thirties and worked on four of The Archers' films prior to *Black Narcissus*, which proved to be his last for them. He later headed the art department of MGM's British studios.

With Percy Day's stunningly realistic paintings of towering ice-capped mountains and far-reaching river valleys enhancing the artistically composed shots of Jack Cardiff, *Black Narcissus* remains one of the most mesmerizingly beautiful color films ever produced. The thirty-two-year-old Cardiff (1914-2009), a former child actor who became a camera assistant at 13, was a rebel when it came to the dos and don'ts of cinematography. He more often chose the "don'ts" in order to capture the effect he sought. In Michael Powell he found a kindred spirit. Together they created the touches necessary for the proper look, such as no facial makeup for the nuns, and the use of arc lights for the pristine exterior shots. Besides being unwieldy, arcs must be strongly diffused with tracing paper, and the dimmer shutters properly manipulated in order to obtain any effect.

The scene where Sister Ruth attempts to push Sister Clodagh off the cliff was actually shot at dawn, the time it occurs in the story. Cardiff used a fog filter to add to the early morning effect, which greatly enhanced its look. The final scene of the film was to take place in the Mother Superior's study in Calcutta. Sister Clodagh explains about the problems she faced at the palace. Speaking in a detached manner, she suddenly notes the compassion in the Mother Superior's eyes and tells the true reason for her failure. The older nun hugs her understandingly, and the picture ends. All the while the rain streaming down the window panes is reflected on the women's faces and the walls.

The last scene actually used was also devised by Cardiff. As the nuns ride down the valley on mules, a close-up of a raindrop hitting a rhubarb leaf in the foreground is followed by a steadily increasing number of drops. After viewing the rushes, director Powell chose that shot over the interior scene to end the film.

The picture's scenes of nuns in their off-white habits flitting about among the shadows in the twisted wind-torn corridors of the palace create an almost jarring counterpoint to the more vibrant outdoor shots. It is also aurally exciting; various types of exotic drums and horns are heard throughout its one-hundred-minute running time, achieving a complete feeling of foreignness. Thomas M. Pryor of *The New York Times* called *Black Narcissus* "...a work of rare pictorial beauty." The Academy of Motion Picture Arts and Sciences obviously agreed, awarding the film Oscars for Cinematography (color), and Art Direction-Set Decoration (color).

For the first time since *Jungle Book*, Sabu's character is his own man. The young general bows to no one; rather, everyone bows to him. Dilip Rai is Prince Azim grown up; Sabu had experienced much of life in a short time, including war, and it shows in the confidence with which he imbues his character. The actor brought a touch of humor as well as

Black Narcissus (Archer Prod./General Film. 1947) Eddie Whaley, Jr., Sabu

dignity to his role. When he first visits the palace he meets with Sister Clodagh to request that he be allowed to attend classes there. He has already drawn up a schedule, which he reads to her and which includes "...algebra with the mathematical sister ... and physics with the physical sister."

Black Narcissus (Archer Prod./General Film, 1947) Jean Simmons, Sabu

While attending classes, he attracts the attention of a young Indian dancing girl (Simmons) whom the nuns have taken in as a favor to Mr. Dean. She follows him about, seducing him with amorous glances. When he refuses to continue a beating of the girl begun by the housekeeper, instead giving her a gold necklace, he is lost. The two run off together, marking the first time that Sabu got the girl, even though they do no more than share a hug on screen. (There are stills of the pair together in poses not seen in the film.)

Soon thereafter the world begins to crumble about the devoted sisters as an infant they had treated dies, an event which turns the people against them. Sister Philippa asks to be transferred, and Sister Ruth's untimely death occurs in rapid succession. And the wind! The incessant, infernal wind continues to blow, mocking their every effort! It all proves too much for the spiritual Christian ladies; their struggle against religious and cultural differences, against the very elements, has been lost. As they pack their bags to return to Calcutta, Dilip Rai returns, dressed to the nines as usual, but all humility inside, apologizing for running away with Kanchi. Sabu makes the most of this brief scene, sounding truly sincere and giving the nuns some solace that their efforts have not completely been in vain.

Black Narcissus was a definite boost to Sabu's career, giving him his first really adult role as well as a production on an artistic par with the films he had made for Alexander Korda. It should have led to offers of more adult roles. But the button-pushers in Hollywood were still surface-oriented, and could not see either beneath Sabu's dark skin or his short height; no such offers came the actor's way. Besides the awards given it, *Black Narcissus* received much press coverage due to censorship problems with the Catholic Legion of Decency in the United States. Originally given a "condemned" rating by that body, it received an "approved for adults" rating after certain footage was deleted and other footage added. The film censor board of Chicago also banned it for the manner in which it portrayed the Anglican nuns, Chicago apparently considering itself a bastion of knowledge regarding the

British Anglican Church. Imagine the condemnation the film would have received if Powell had used the original religious order as elucidated by the author in her book. For it was none other than Roman Catholic sisters who are seduced by the forces of Satan on the rooftop of the world. Powell wisely changed all this and let the Anglican Church take it on the chin.

On July 7, 1947, a special invitational premiere of the film was held at the Carthay Circle Theater in Los Angeles. Sabu was in attendance, along with Deborah Kerr, J. Arthur Rank, and many other stars. Despite the censorship controversy, *Black Narcissus* was well received by critics. Sabu's work was hardly mentioned, even though he was billed second behind Kerr, and the trailer for the picture had termed him "The Exotic Star of Two Worlds", a tribute to his status and his importance to the production. *Variety* rather derisively commented: "A difficult subject has been tactfully handled"; "The cast has been well chosen..."; and "...Sabu, who plays the young general as though he were Sabu." Leslie Halliwell, in his *Film Guide*, called *Black Narcissus* "A visual and emotional stunner, despite some narrative uncertainty." Even noted film historian Leonard Maltin fails to mention Sabu, while calling the picture, "Visually sumptuous, dramatically charged... one of the most breathtaking color films ever made..." This could very well be due to the fact that Sabu has but ten minutes of screen time, and his character of the young general does little to advance the plot. At one point his character mentions that his cologne, "Black Narcissus", came from the Army and Navy stores in London. This is the one link to home that the sisters experience in the otherwise totally alien environment, hence its use as the title.

Black Narcissus was the last truly exceptional film in which Sabu would appear; the next sixteen years and fourteen films brought only fair and poor scripts and mostly low production values. But it was a different world now. The changed situation wrought by the shattering devastation of World War II forced everyone to view life with a jaundiced eye as Romanticism became passé. While *Black Narcissus* was in the editing stage, Michael Powell's editor on *The Edge of the World*, Derek Twist (1905-1979), presented him with an idea for a picture set in Brazil based on a 1940 novel by Desmond Holdridge, *Death of a Common Man* (*The End of the River* was the U.S. title). Powell shared Twist's enthusiasm, and raised the money necessary for a trip to Brazil for research and background material.

While there, Twist's discovery in Rio de Janeiro of a very attractive celebrity named Bibi Ferreira (b. 1922) increased his optimism for the project's success. Only 24, she was already running her own theater company, the Phoenix, in Rio de Janeiro. She was signed to play the female lead opposite Sabu, who had completed his work on *Black Narcissus*. He and the British members of the cast assembled their gear and were off to the largest country in South America to make *The End of the River*, with a screenplay supervised by Emeric Pressburger. It was all to little avail. As Michael Powell recalled in *A Life in Movies*, "The actors did their best, but it was all uphill when it should have been downstream. Even Esmond Knight as the heavy, even Sabu as the hero, couldn't save it."

The End of the River (The Archers/Rank, 1947) Sabu

The story concerns a young Arekuna Indian named Manoel (Sabu), whose family has been wronged by a local chieftain. Failing to take revenge, the young man becomes an outcast from his tribe and is forced into the white man's world. Initially given a job on a boat by a kindly white man, he falls prey to scheming whites once he leaves. Though he had married a bi-racial woman he had met on the boat, she too proves equally ignorant of "civilization". Meeting up with a recruiter for a leftist workmen's union, Manoel accepts the job supplied by them, being deceived by the comparatively high wages. When the union's activities turn to violence, Manoel is arrested along with the others. Later released, he finds all doors closed to him for having been a member of the union. Finding a position at last, he is recognized by his fellow workers and harassed. This torment is so severe it causes Manoel to become delusionary; he imagines another ex-union member to be the chieftain who had begun all his troubles, and kills him with a baling hook. Arrested for murder, Manoel is released by a merciful judge after a series of character witnesses show how he was victimized first by the chieftain, and later by the white men. Manoel and his wife then settle on a piece of land at "the end of the river", a fertile area where they are able to live in peace. Except for the later *Mistress of the World*, *The End of the River* is the most atypical of Sabu's films. It is frequently depressing in its depiction of realistic conditions, and the famous Sabu smile is seldom seen. With the likes of Esmond Knight, Torin Thatcher, and Robert Douglas in support, the film is well-acted. Bibi Ferreira adds what little brightness there is in this gloomy tale, with her gentle ways and pleasant singing voice, but the overall mood is somber.

Sabu was again believable in his role, for his features and skin tone allowed him to portray people of many lands - Arabs, Polynesians, South Americans, Mexicans, Native Americans and, of course, Indians.

Twist chose to present the story out of chronological sequence, beginning with Manoel in jail for murder. As the Indian tells his story, the first flashback occurs; with each witness, another flashback is shown, until Manoel's entire recent history is related. Aided by the use of folk songs, the score is often upbeat, and the photography by

Christopher Challis is exceptional, offering a combination documentary/film noir style. Despite the high production values, the story lacks excitement, the only suspense being the outcome of Manoel's trial. As a vehicle for Sabu, it strayed too far afield from his established milieus to satisfy his fans, with the added onus of failing to allow him to stretch as an actor, as such a project should have done. Even *Black Narcissus*, with its realistic characters, at least possessed an otherworldly quality due to its setting.

Presenting the story as he did, Twist pleased some viewers and irked others. While Irene Thirer of *The New York Post* wrote: "...there is plentiful melodramatic action set against provocative backgrounds..." Thomas M. Pryor of *The New York Times* complained: "*The End of the River* has been brightly photographed...but it is a frightfully dull and rambling movie." Such criticism could hardly stimulate attendance; the film did very poor business and is seldom seen today. By the time *The End of the River* was completed, The Archers were deeply involved with *The Red Shoes*, which became the quintessential film about ballet.

With his work completed on *The End of the River*, Sabu could not wait to leave Brazil. Not bothering to watch the remainder of the filming, he made an immediate beeline for California. Once home, the World War II veteran found himself without work. Like many stars, he waited for a new project to be offered him, although he knew the results of his recently completed film would not do much for his box-office record or popularity.

Chapter Eleven
Love and Marriage

With World War II ended, scientists and technicians were again free to create and develop products with peaceful uses, some of which had been invented before the war. Among the latter was television (the British Broadcasting Corporation had begun public service in London in 1936), which proved to be anything but peaceful as far as film studio heads were concerned. Once technology made the invention affordable to the general public and television antennas began sprouting like weeds on the nation's rooftops, there was much fear and anxiety in Hollywood as box-office receipts took a precipitous drop after a peak year in 1946.

Adding to that apprehension was a Supreme Court decision handed down in May of 1948, stating that the major studios were guilty of monopolistic methods by their block-booking of films (the selling of a full season's output of films, sight unseen, to an exhibitor on one contract) and the fixing of admission prices. These practices were declared illegal and the studios were forced to sell off their theater chains, which constituted a major source of income and gave the studios a guaranteed outlet for their product. This resulted in a domino effect; since the studios no longer owned the theaters, they were compelled to cut back on their output, thereby reducing the number of actors on their payrolls. Those immediately affected were the big-name stars commanding large salaries whose drawing power had diminished due either to aging or inability to adapt their pre-war images to post-war trends. Some fled to Europe, where they were still popular. The ones who remained in Hollywood were not offered new contracts and settled for substantial pay cuts when offered work by independent producers. The latter saw their opportunity to make substantial profits on pictures costing much less than the studio product, which always included a sizable "overhead".

Among these producers was one Monty Shaff, who was readying a production based on a popular non-fiction work entitled *Man-Eaters of Kumaon* by James Corbett, a renowned big-game hunter. Set in India, the book deals with the hunter's harrowing experiences with Bengal tigers. Given the setting, Shaff naturally sought out Sabu for the starring role. He sold the now freelancing actor on the idea by promising that the end result would be a super production. He next tried to get Jean Simmons on loan from J. Arthur Rank for the part of the Hindu girl. Fortunately for the young actress, who had played an Indian girl in *Black Narcissus* the year before, Rank refused to lend her, saving her from being typecast in such roles and allowing her to enjoy a fruitful career in Hollywood.

As it turned out, Shaff's "super production" was hastily contrived from background footage shot in India by the film's technical advisor, Major M.H. Whyte, Indian Army, retired, who had spent seventeen years on the sub-continent. The actual filming was done at the General Services Studio in Hollywood. Hunter/writer Corbett still made his home in India and supplied some equipment and costumes for the production. Two sets were specially constructed at the studio, one a village with terraced wheat fields surrounded by a cyclorama depicting the Himalayas, and the other a pair of twenty-foot-high cages, one for the tigers and one for the camera crew. A few scenes were shot in nearby Simi Valley for good measure.

The sparse plot concerns an American doctor (Wendell Corey) who had been more concerned with his income than his bedside manner. Tiring of the medical scene, he journeys to India to hunt tigers and hopefully discover his true vocation. During his sojourn he wounds a tiger, which subsequently kills several natives and causes a young woman (Joanne Page) to miscarry. The latter is the wife of the future chief of her village, Narain (Sabu). The accident also ends her child-bearing capability, and as the chief's wife is expected to produce a male heir she now knows this to be impossible and decides to sacrifice herself as bait for the man-eater. Hearing this, the doctor, already racked with guilt, sets out to stop her. Arriving just in time to prevent the beast from attacking the girl, he is himself clawed to death, but not before killing the tiger with a knife.

Sabu had little to do in the film except obey his father, till the fields, and express concern over his wife. From that standpoint, Corey (1914-1968) should have been given star billing, but Sabu had the bigger name.

The finished product, which was released through Universal, fooled no one, including critic Bosley Crowther of *The New York Times*, who called *Man-Eater of Kumaon* "...a standard studio-made jungle yarn...."; others were more angered. A critic with the very formidable appellation of Mozelle Britton Dinehart, writing in *Nite-Life* magazine, charged to defend Sabu after viewing this limited effort: "Sabu is one of the few colorful personalities left in Hollywood. It seems extremely unfortunate to pay heavy tariff for his name value and then fail to use him to advantage when there was every opportunity to do so. Though given top billing, Sabu came off third best when the roles were passed out and the fans are going to squawk plenty." Continuing, he stated: "...but Sabu, who stands for the epitome of jungle lore in audience minds, is allowed to drive the tiger away from captivity through clumsiness and is sent into the wheat fields to labor while Corey and Joanne capture the man-eater!"

Sabu did a promotional spot for the production over radio station KWIK in the San Fernando Valley to no avail; box-office receipts proved only fair.

Before *Man-Eater of Kumaon*'s release in July of 1948, Sabu received an offer from Columbia Pictures to star in their latest project, *Song of India*. He was still the one called whenever an "A" picture set either in India or a jungle requiring a native lead was to be produced. With Gail Russell (1924-1961) and Turhan Bey as the other stars, filming began early that summer. Work progressed smoothly until Miss Russell suddenly took ill. At that point, filming around her was impossible, so a double was sought for the ailing actress. One was found in the person of a very lovely bright-eyed brunette actress/model /singer named Marilyn Cooper.

Miss Cooper had been the top model at Warner Bros., posing for statuary and paintings used in various films, after a brief career as a singer with Bob Crosby's band and a stint in the USO during the war. A native of West Virginia, she had also appeared on Broadway in the popular wartime musical *Panama Hattie* and had had a small role in Orson Welles' much-maligned production of *Macbeth* (1948) over at Republic. When called by Columbia, she had no idea of what was in store for her. After a quick check by a casting director, she was deemed "perfect" and ushered into the makeup department. While she was being tended to and fussed over, Sabu walked in and introduced himself, explaining to Marilyn that she would be working with him. By her own admission, Marilyn's heart began beating wildly at that moment. She had followed Sabu's career since its beginning and now found the young star most attractive through the thrill of actually meeting him. The feeling turned out to be mutual; Sabu showed his solicitude one day on location when he noticed that Marilyn was skipping lunch because she was the only woman present. He hired a man to pole a raft along a river while he shared his lunch with the shy actress. They began dating as soon as filming on *Song of India* was finished. Sabu was thoroughly smitten. He told his good friend Bud Knight that Marilyn was the girl for him and shortly thereafter proposed to her. She put him off for almost three months, but finally succumbed to his charm, and on October 19, 1948, they eloped and were wed in a private ceremony at St. Nicholas Episcopal Church in Encino. Sabu phoned Shaik to tell him the good news, asking that no one else be told yet. Shaik promised, but that night phoned all the Hollywood columnists with the story. Now married, Marilyn selflessly ended her show-business career, being determined to make a perfect home for herself and her new spouse.

Sabu's brother ceased handling his affairs around this time, deciding to go into business for himself. Sabu set him up with his own furniture store in 1950. The two remained close, visiting each other frequently.

Song of India did not fare as well as its star and stand-in (for that is what Miss Cooper actually was; she was photographed only from behind, in long shot, or with her face hidden by a wide-brimmed hat, and received no credit for her work). Sabu was once again a jungle dweller, this time in a sacred jungle which is invaded by the prince of the region's royal family seeking animal specimens for zoos. The jungle inhabitants have been peacefully co-existing with the animals for centuries and forbid anyone to hunt there. The prevailing superstition is that one human must die for every animal killed or captured. The Prince (Bey) and Princess Tara (Russell) ignore the warnings of Ramdar (Sabu), and continue to capture animals. Ramdar sneaks into the camp one night and frees them; he later takes Tara hostage, but the Prince counters by threatening to kill a number of Ramdar's people unless she is returned safely. Ramdar leads his captive to a plateau overlooking the entire area and as he shows the princess the sacred jungle, he is attacked by a tiger which had been wounded by the prince and suffers a badly mauled left arm. The Prince trails the couple, and calls off his soldiers from Ramdar's village when he sees that Tara is safe. Ramdar again asks him to abandon his expedition. The Prince responds by challenging our wounded hero to a knife fight. Ramdar seems doomed, but the tiger reappears; the Prince fires at the beast and they both plunge over the cliff.

Ramdar, apparently finding a copy of Burke's Peerage, turns out to be the last in line of the former ruling family of the province. He suddenly opts for

Song of India (Columbia, 1949) Sabu, Gail Russell, Turhan Bey

the good life, and at the end of the film he rides off with Princess Tara in an elegant automobile, wearing an even more elegant outfit.

All this was directed in rather uninspired fashion by Albert S. Rogell (1901-1987), a veteran director of second features. Wrote Thomas M. Pryor of *The New York Times*: "*Song of India* runs its commonplace course without causing any excitement." *Variety* thought a little better of this production, stating: "Here is another jungle adventure thriller of the Sabu Elephant Boy - Jungle Book pattern, with Turhan Bey added for good measure." Of *Song of India*'s star, the trade paper added, "Sabu carries out the role of jungle prince with dignity." Despite the added detail of sepia tinting, the film's earnings were less than respectable. Production values for *Song of India* were excellent, but due to the picture's performance at the box office, it became the last American movie which starred Sabu that gave him full support. From his following film to his final appearance, only the foreign pictures and the last two American movies, in which he had supporting roles, received decent treatment.

With a beautiful, loving and very devoted wife now at his side, Sabu was more than ready to brave any challenges brought by a new decade and changing film fashions. Marilyn's support was to prove vital in the often trying years ahead; whenever the going got tough, she was always there for her husband.

Chapter Twelve

Europe and India

Sabu now felt that he had three strikes against him: the failure of his last three films, his having attained full manhood with its attendant loss of boyish charm, and the changing tastes of the movie-going public, which meant that fantasy and jungle epics were currently out of favor.

Not one to remain inactive, he now felt it would be pragmatic to consider other means of making a living. Toward that end he began investing in real estate. He also started a contracting business and constructed several apartment buildings in the Los Angeles area. All that while he and Marilyn continued living in the colonial-style house he had purchased while in the service, which Shaik had found for him as a twenty-first birthday present. Located in the Northridge Estates section of the then remote Los Angeles suburb of Chatsworth, the property included verdant lawns and a large freshwater lake.

With an adoring wife at his side, and a good income

from both his business and investments, Sabu was no longer overly concerned about his future in films, although he was open to offers. What he was not prepared for was the paternity suit filed against him in late May of 1949.

Sabu's first experience with the dark side of celebrity life in America was instigated by a young British ballet dancer who accused him of siring her illegitimate eight-month-old daughter. The trial did not take place until mid-October 1950. After it was revealed that the plaintiff had had several affairs and could not even prove the child to be hers, it took a Superior Court jury comprised of six men and six women less than three hours to bring in a "not guilty" verdict. Both a retrial and an appeal were denied the dancer by the same court, and the case was officially closed in December 1950. However, in March of 1952, the District Court of Appeals granted the dancer's request for a new trial on the grounds that the Superior Court judge had given "erroneous and prejudicial" instructions to the jury during the first trial. Happily for Sabu and Marilyn, the outcome of the second trial was the same as that of the first.

To add to his troubles, just one month following the first trial, the top floor of Sabu's two-story home was destroyed by fire while he and Marilyn were on vacation. Only a week before, the actor had reported to the district attorney's office that ever since the paternity trial, attempts had been made to frighten his expectant wife and prowlers had been seen on the property. Now, after a check of the fire-damaged premises, Sabu discovered that a number of valuables was missing. As expected, his insurance company paid for the damage. But two years later an alleged acquaintance of the star received a jail term after confessing to having torched the house as a favor to Sabu. Sabu totally denied the allegation, but his insurance company filed suit against him for close to $20,000. It was two frustrating years before the star was again acquitted, this time of committing arson "by act, design, or procurement."

After removing the remains of his first home, the popular actor built an eight-room ranch house on the same site. This time he made sure to include enough space for his growing collection of elephant figurines sent by his many fans around the world, as well as for his antique silver and china collections.

The year 1951 also proved eventful. On January 2, Marilyn gave birth to their first child, a handsome six-pound, three-ounce baby boy, whom the couple named Paul. A short time later, during dinner at Ciro's one evening, Sabu was approached by an agent from Lippert Pictures with an offer for a film. Formerly Screen Guild Productions, Lippert specialized in producing low-budget features with short running times as well as releasing films of independent producers. It had been well over a year since Sabu had been before a camera; he agreed, without even reading the script. When he did, his enthusiasm quickly dwindled, but since he had made a verbal commitment, he went through with it.

The result was a seventy-minute feature called *Savage Drums*, a product of its time, that is to say, anti-Communist to the core.

A fictional island in the Pacific Ocean is threatened with takeover by Red Chinese forces after the king is assassinated while visiting his younger brother Tipo (Sabu), who of all things is studying at a prestigious American university to become a boxer. Tipo returns to his homeland, where his evil Marxist cousin has begun paving the way for Communist rule. Tipo, now king, tries to get the ruling council to agree to signing a protective treaty with the U.S., but is thwarted by his cousin, who then attempts to poison him. Communist troops invade the capital; Tipo organizes resistance, and the Reds are defeated in a fiercely fought battle. The protective treaty is signed, and Tipo takes a gorgeous native girl as his queen. While the plot remains below Shakespearean standards, Sabu's track record with the ladies continued to improve, as he got the girl for the fourth time in his last five films. Everything about this film is average, from the uninspired script to the direction. The limp comic relief is provided by Sid Melton (b. 1920) and Bob Easton (b. 1930) as a couple of all-American types. Longtime movie veteran H.B. Warner (1876-1958) appears as the king's advisor and winds up with a Communist bul-

let in his chest for
his trouble. Steven
Geray (1899-1974)
is convincing as the
chief heavy, and
Francis Pierlot (1875-
1955) stands out as a
blind islander. Sabu
must have had flash-
backs to his war ex-

Savage Drums (Lippert, 1951) Lobby card

perience, as he mans both a machine gun and a Thompson
submachine gun in the climactic battle, in which "right"
(our side) triumphs over "wrong" (their side).

Variety's reviewer thought little of this programmer,
calling it "...a routine melodrama. Good title and name
of Sabu supply some selling help..." "Picture started with
a bad script by Fenton Earnshaw, and neither producer-
director William Berke nor the players are able to raise it
above mediocrity...Sabu rates better material," he added.

Soon thereafter, a different and better offer came Sabu's way, the novelty of which intrigued him. It also allowed the harried actor a chance to leave his recent troubles behind. Making the offer was a British entrepreneur
named Tom Arnold, owner of the Harringay Circus, who
was in the process of signing up the finest circus acts in
the world for the upcoming season. He wanted Sabu for
the elephant act (surprise, surprise!) and offered him top

billing along with a generous contract. Accepting the job without hesitation, the Sabus were soon on their way to England with infant son in tow.

Being a circus star proved an exhilarating experience for the veteran movie actor. Nattily attired in white shirt, scarlet vest, white jodhpurs, shiny black boots, and adorned with his trademark turban, Sabu cut a dashing figure as he rode into the center ring of the Harringay Arena in London during the Christmas holidays. Unfortunately, his audience preferred to see him as they had back in 1937, clad only in a simple *dhoty*. Bowing to public pressure almost caused Sabu to catch pneumonia, but at least he was allowed to keep his turban.

The elephants proved something of a problem at first, too, as they were selected from different groups. They fought among themselves, refusing to obey their master and wandering off in all directions. It did not take long for "The Elephant Boy" to straighten them out. The popular personality also appeared in "Arabian Nights", described in the circus program as "a grand spectacle".

While Sabu was in England, Robert Flaherty, the founding father of the documentary film genre, passed away on July 23, 1951, at the age of sixty-seven. A year later his numerous admirers among the British intelligentsia got together and devised a radio tribute to him. It was broadcast by the BBC on September 2, 1952, and entitled *Portrait of Robert Flaherty*.

Narrated by Duncan MacIntyre, it included fellow documentarian John Grierson, actress Lillian Gish, French artist Henri Matisse, French filmmaker Jean Renoir, actor/directors Erich von Stroheim, John Huston, Orson Welles, and, of course, Sir Alexander Korda.

Sabu was interviewed, and two of his recollections of the warmly-remembered filmmaker were included in the broadcast. He emphasized Flaherty's paternal attitude toward him, stating: "...to me he was just like a father..." Recalling his disposition, Sabu stated, "...He was very cheerful all the time. No matter what went wrong or what had to be done, he was always the same, cheerful."

While the Harringay Circus was preparing for a European tour, Sabu received an offer to appear in a film with the very popular Italian star Vittorio De Sica (1902-1974). It was a comedy entitled *Buongiorno, Elefante!* (*Hello, Elephant!*), being made by Rizzoli Film, and was released in Italy in 1952 and in the U.S. in 1954. Billed second behind De Sica, Sabu was more of a guest star, appearing only in the middle section of the picture.

Vittorio plays an underpaid elementary school teacher with four children, under threat of eviction for back rent. When an expected raise fails to materialize, he plans a strike. Sabu, as an Indian prince, appears out of the blue at a Roman ruin and De Sica hires him as a guide. After viewing several sites in Rome, the two stop at a church containing a saint's relic. Constantly seeking souvenirs, and not

understanding Western customs, the prince pilfers the sacred relic. Later, at the teacher's apartment, Sabu saves Vittorio from eviction by paying the back rent to the landlord,
who had already rented the apartment to a young couple.
Sabu promptly charms the young wife and is caught kissing
her; a big change from his Hollywood films, where his skin
color prevented him from being much more than a friend
to a female. Sabu next turns on the charm with De Sica's
children, singing a lullaby (which is dubbed, like his speaking voice) and playing with them. He gives the relic to the
youngest child, but De Sica takes it away from her and sur-
reptitiously returns it to the church. Having obtained the
license number of the prince's car from a bystander, the
police trail him to the teacher's apartment and apprehend
him, only to release him when he is identified as the Sultan
of Nagore. Having done his good deeds, the ruler returns
to his homeland.

Some time later, a baby elephant is delivered to the
teacher, a gift from the sultan. The animal's arrival causes
a great stir in the building, eventually forcing De Sica to
dispose of it. He has no luck until he goes to a convent,
where the Mother Superior refuses to keep the beast at
first, but relents when De Sica counters with, "There's
nothing left to do but give it to the Communists. What
a shame! They'll make such propaganda out of it." Vittorio leads the teacher's strike to a successful conclusion.
Returning home, he finds that the elephant has escaped

from the convent and is at the apartment building. Fortunately, the manager of the local zoo is there, too, and he buys the beast for a handsome sum. This tides the teacher over until his pay raise is voted on favorably.

Sabu's character was used to move the plot along and add much needed color to the otherwise ordinary events which make up the proceedings. He appears from nowhere, and seemingly returns there after serving his purpose. He looked good, though his outfit was strictly bargain basement material. An interesting detail concerns the film's other titles: *Pardon My Trunk*, and *Sabu, Prince of Thieves*, the latter suggesting that his role may originally have been larger. Whatever the case, Sabu did a creditable job in his fourth and final performance as an Indian of royal blood.

Hello, Elephant! gained much from De Sica's gentle presence as well. Highly regarded as both a director and an actor, the popular star was then in mid-career, possessing as much of his own brand of charm as Sabu. The film is well photographed and the lightness of the score perfectly suits the action. Gianni Franciolini's direction makes good use of Roman landmarks. Of this production, Bosley Crowther of *The New York Times* had the following to say: "...a minor debauch of Italian sentiment and whimsy..." and "Except for Signor De Sica, the only recognizable actor is Sabu, who makes a few pseudo-regal passes as the Indian potentate."

Meanwhile, the Harringay Circus toured the Continent after its highly successful season in Britain. Movie and circus fans in Germany, France and Holland turned out by the thousands to see the world-famous "Elephant Boy" in person. As it happened, his earlier films such as *The Thief of Bagdad* and *Jungle Book*, as well as his Universal features, long delayed by World War II, were just reaching those countries and proved just as popular as when first released. Older moviegoers, who no doubt remembered Sabu's first two films, which had been made before the war, also turned out in large numbers.

During breaks from the circus, Sabu would take Marilyn and Paul on car trips around Europe. They frequently visited out-of-the-way towns and villages and were often invited by the local citizenry to dine in their homes. One winter they drove across the Alps into Switzerland and got snowed in while visiting Zoltan Korda and his family at their abode in Lucerne. While he had been a frequent visitor to Korda's Beverly Hills home, this winter interlude marked the first time that the film star had visited his favorite director at his European residence.

The spring of 1953 found Sabu touring with the Harringay Circus for the last time. When that company folded its tents and returned to England, the actor remained in northern Italy. He was immediately snapped up by German impresario Frans Mikkenie for his circus and soon began traveling again. That tour ended in the spring of

1954, when the popular star received another film proposal, this time from Venturini Film of Italy.

The film was *Il Tesoro Del Bengala* (*The Treasure of
Bengal*), an old-fashioned adventure yarn which kept Sabu
busy with more action scenes than he had had for years.
Made during the summer of 1954, *Il Tesoro Del Bengala*
proved popular enough to gross twice as much as his De
Sica picture. Sabu fans in the United States had to wait
two years before it was released there. (It should be noted
here that this film was released in the U.S. under the title
The Treasure of Bengal, not *Jungle Hell*, as some reference works state; the latter is a separate film which was
made in the U.S.)

Sabu looked good, as usual, and handled his unde-
manding role with enthusiasm, despite receiving only fair
direction. He played a village fisherman in this tale set
in 17th-century India. The local temple houses a great
ruby known as "The Light of Vishnu", which is sought
by Portuguese slave traders operating in the area. They
make a deal with the headman of the village to trade guns
for the jewel. With the guns the latter plans to rule the
entire valley. Ainur (Sabu) discovers his treachery when
the headman tries to prevent Ainur's marriage to his be-
trothed, Karima (Luisa Boni) and does his utmost to thwart
him. After several adventures he succeeds, revealing the
headman's perfidy to the people and slaying him in a duel
fought with scimitars.

Better direction and editing could have made this a more enjoyable film, but the lack of camera movement and too many drawn-out scenes prevent it from being so. The voices are appropriate, but the English dialogue leans toward American slang with its liberal use of contractions, and the dubbing is only fair. One of the film's highlights is a dance performed in the temple by a septet of comely adolescent girls, who leap about brandishing swords in an extremely graceful and well-choreographed number. An interesting sidelight is that the headman is also played by an Indian actor, Ananda Koumar.

The costumes are colorful and appear authentic; Sabu again wears a turban and is almost bare-chested, wearing nothing but short vests on his upper body. The only wild animal he appears with is a tiger that has gastronomic designs on him. While a composer is credited for the score, most of the music is lifted directly from Erich Wolfgang Korngold's scores for *The Adventures of Robin Hood* and *The Sea Hawk*. The music also stops abruptly at crucial moments, to the viewer's puzzlement. *Motion Picture Exhibitor* for April 18, 1956, cared little for it, however, stating: "Confusion reigns supreme in this weak import. Mayhaps the name of Sabu still may mean something, but on the whole it's just filler for the indiscriminate. The acting, direction and production are just fair."

The next project offered to Sabu must have delighted him no end, for it came from his homeland, India. So from

Rome, he, Marilyn and Paul headed east in October 1953, taking their beloved Cadillac with them. Arriving ahead of schedule, they toured Bangalore, Mysore and Malabar. Much ado was made over the return of India's most renowned celebrity, although after Sabu had been there some time the newspapers began negatively reporting that he had become so Americanized in his dress and speech that Marilyn was more a daughter of India than he was a son. They also assumed that Sabu had forgotten how to speak Urdu. He played along with this except when he was overcharged for something, when he would suddenly reveal a startling fluency in that ancient tongue. The trio stayed in a forest outside of Bangalore, the largest city in Mysore, roughing it in roomy tents, attending balls and feasts given by various maharajas. They even observed a *keddah* like the one in *Elephant Boy*. It was arranged by the new Maharaja of Mysore, the son of the man who provided little Selar Shaik with a pension after the death of the boy's father in the early thirties.

While Sabu and Marilyn were guests of the maharaja, they were made honorary members of his family in tribute to the world-wide success of Mysore's most famous native son. While in Bangalore, Marilyn rubbed shoulders with then-Vice President Richard Nixon, when both were shopping in the same store for brass goods. When filming was due to begin, Sabu journeyed north to Bombay to appear in a black-and-white fantasy picture for Falcon

Films called *Baghdad,* which was released in 1954. Unfortunately, this film is not available for appraisal.

During his sojourn in his homeland, Sabu saw things he had been unaware of as a child in Mysore. He later told friends the extremes of wealth and poverty had upset him greatly, making him more appreciative than ever of his American citizenship and the special opportunities that had been granted him. His work on *Baghdad* completed, Sabu was tested for a role in *Mother India,* a major film to be directed by Mehboob Khan, one of India's leading filmmakers. However, he was not accepted for the part in that picture, which was released in 1957.

After six months on the sub-continent, thoughts of home began to loom large in the minds of Sabu and Marilyn. They had spent the better part of four years touring Europe, besides the Indian interlude, and were now more than a little homesick. Before they were ready to depart, however, letters arrived regarding important business matters in California, and it was decided that Marilyn and Paul should return home first. Sabu followed a month later, exhilarated by the reception he had received everywhere in Europe and in India, and with three more motion pictures to his credit, as well as some hard-earned circus experience. The spring of 1955 found the travel-weary family together again, happily ensconced back in Chatsworth.

Chapter Thirteen
Home to Hollywood

With his very successful European tour added to his list of accomplishments, Sabu settled in back home with Marilyn and his son Paul, now four years old. Feeling that his career had been revitalized, he began sifting through the movie and television scripts which continued to flow in to the house in Chatsworth. Unsurprisingly, he encountered the same tunnel vision mentality that existed before he left. Not one of the proposals he received offered him anything more than "jungle boy" roles. The best among them was a widescreen film along the lines of *Elephant Boy* for the Cinerama corporation, for which Sabu made a brief return to India seeking suitable locations. Developed by former MGM studio head Louis B. Mayer, then advisor to Cinerama, the project was still in preparation at the time of Mayer's death in October 1957. With his passing, the production was shelved, never to be realized. Legal costs from the arson case having made a severe dent in his finances, Sabu knew he had to make some sort of choice among the proffered projects, so he began separating the wheat from the chaff. The problem was in finding *any* wheat amidst the chaff.

Among the many offers was one from fellow former child star Mickey Rooney (b. 1920). The one-time MGM mainstay now had his own company, Mickey Rooney Enterprises, and had plans for a television series with a working title of The *Magic Lamp*. Wanting to shoot it in color in India, Rooney sought Sabu to be his star. Sabu agreed, signing an exclusive television contract to appear in twenty-six half-hour episodes, as reported in the June 25, 1954, issue of *Variety*. Before anyone could say "Gunga Din", though, the money ran out and the series was never made.

Rooney, now a producer at Republic Pictures, next developed a project with a South American setting. Needing an established name in order to obtain backing for the picture, Mickey again approached Sabu. This time a picture was actually made. Entitled *Jaguar,* the story concerned a young man descended from a fierce Amazon tribe, but raised in civilization by a British scientist. The man, Juano (Sabu), fears that he will revert to their savage ways, which include donning jaguar skins and clawing their enemies to death. He becomes involved with two Americans, played by veteran heavy Barton MacLane (1902-1969) and newcomer Touch [later Mike] Connors (b.

1925), who play on his fears to cover their nefarious aims. When some gruesome murders occur, Juano feels guilty and returns to his tribe. This conflict from which he suffers is the lone interesting idea in the film. The rest had all been seen before. Sabu does get to fight a python and a jaguar, and is allowed a love interest in the person of the scientist's secretary, Rita, played by the very lovely and ever-popular Chiquita (1938-2003). All is resolved when the real murderer is condemned to "sleep with the fishes" (in this case, piranhas) and Juano and Rita return to civilization. Released in mid-September of 1956, *Jaguar* failed to draw the requisite number of people away from their television sets in order to achieve much box-office interest. Sabu's old nemesis, *Variety*, was, for once, somewhat kind to him, as its reviewer wrote: "This routine yarn about murderous jaguar-men in the Amazon jungle has the sole advantage of Sabu's name for the less discriminating program market," but noted that the film "has little regard for entertainment value or story construction..."

Sabu next agreed to star in a film made by Ron and June Ormond for the Howco organization. The Ormonds had been making films for over a decade, beginning with "B" westerns and musicals. The couple then began arranging personal appearance tours for minor movie stars, who traveled the nation's hinterlands with great success. By the time of their association with Sabu, they had moved on to science-fiction films, which had become very popular in the post-war period. For the famous "Elephant Boy". however, the pair concocted another jungle tale. Called *The Black Panther*, the story borrowed so many elements from *Song of India* as to be a virtual clone of the earlier film.

Sabu is again the lord of a jungle region, responsible for the wellbeing of the inhabitants, both quadruped and biped. Along comes yet another maharaja, shooting ani-mals for sport. The same ruler also tries to wed an already engaged farmer's daughter. Sabu pre-vents the latter oc-currence, then de-feats the maharaja in a fight, sparing his life in exchange

The Black Panther
(Howco, 1956) Title card

for the rajah's promise never to return to the jungle. The script also contained a bit of Kipling; Sabu is alleged to have been raised by animals, and the opening and closing narration refer to "the Laws of the Jungle", to wit: "Now these are the Laws of the Jungle, and many and mighty are they, but the head and the hoof, and the haunch and the hump of the Law is - Obey!"; "So this is the Law of the Jungle, as old and as true as the sky. And all that shall keep it may prosper, but the one that shall break it must die." These lines paraphrase those of Kipling's "The Law of the Jungle" from *The Second Jungle Book*. Released late in 1956, with a running time of only twenty-six minutes, *The Black Panther* is the third and last short in which Sabu appeared.

Not long after its completion, the Ormonds showed how highly they thought of the film. Wanting to break free of Howco, they traded their interest in one of their old westerns for *The Black Panther* minus Sabu's footage. This must have left all of five minutes. Ron Ormond had bought some film of a boy supposedly raised by gorillas. Combining the two, they added footage of a girl raised by gorillas, released it as *Untamed Mistress*, and were well on their way in the wonderful world of exploitation films.

Howco had distributed *The Black Panther* with the Sabu footage, but failed to pay the Ormonds their share of the profits, claiming that the Sabu footage still belonged to the company. A resulting lawsuit was eventually settled to the satisfaction of both parties.

Despite this disrespectful treatment, and the film's shortcomings, *The Black Panther* was not the worst film Sabu ever appeared in; that dubious honor was reserved for the next production in which he appeared.

By the mid-fifties, the old Hollywood studio system was tottering on its last legs. Independent producers increasingly hovered about, picture deals in hand, poised and ready to pounce on the latest star to have his or her contract suddenly terminated. Some of these producers actually knew something about filmmaking, although most did not. They often had the money and the physical equipment necessary to make a movie; what they lacked were skill and talent. Among these industry bottom-dwellers was an outfit calling itself Taj Mahal Productions. Its origins are obscure, and should deservedly remain so.

Sometime in 1956, Taj Mahal coaxed Sabu into starring in their initial production, which they represented as a *Jungle Book* remake. After Sabu's scenes were shot, the producers reached either a creative or financial crisis, or both, and panicked. Desperate to have a finished film, they added much inappropriate stock footage to achieve a viable running time. The resulting disaster, called *Jungle Hell*, made Ed Wood's *Glen Or Glenda?* look like *Citizen Kane*. It is truly one of the finest examples ever made of how *not* to make a movie. *Jungle Hell* cannot seem to make up its mind what type of picture it is - jungle, science fiction or documentary. Elements of all three are mixed in with the skill of a master butcher.

Before the film opens, a pompous expression of gratitude from the producers to the Government of India and the Maharaja of Mysore appears against the crest of Mysore. Had anyone in that venerable land seen the outcome of their hospitality, it would undoubtedly have meant war, or at least major skirmishes, between the United States and India.

The film begins with stock footage of Indian landmarks,

accompanied by poorly recorded narration. The picture then meanders to the story, which concerns a strange stone that burns anyone who touches it. The small jungle village is inhabited by Sabu, his nephew (played by son Paul), his sister-in-law, and two shifty-looking reprobates. The stone is reported to have fallen from the sky. Having digested this, the viewer is next treated to a series of mismatched studio and location shots featuring more elephants than a Republican convention. Shots of a tacky-looking flying saucer are occasionally interspersed, from which beams of light issue, presumably aimed earthward. Their purpose, if any, like that of the movie itself, remains a mystery.

An American scientist (David Bruce) attempts to discover the nature of the rock with the aid of a female scientist (K.T. Stevens) sent out from London. Veteran character actor George E. Stone (1903-1967) adds to these proceedings by playing an individual of indeterminate origin, whose every action is inexplicable. At least he is mercifully dispatched by a tiger before the picture ends. Whether or not any of them succeed at anything is not made clear, for the same garbled voiceover soon closes the film against more shots of landmarks.

For the first time in his now-faltering career, Sabu had been cheated. Fortunately, he had not signed a contract, so he was able to sue the producers for illegal use of his name. With the movie itself as damning evidence, he easily won his case.

The happy result was that *Jungle Hell* was never released theatrically. However, a company known as Medallion TV showed extremely poor taste by buying it, for the print owned by this writer bears their logo. So apparently this production, not fit even for a cutting room floor, occasionally airs very late at night somewhere in this Goldwyn-forsaken land of ours. Since no record of Taj Mahal Productions seems to exist, it must be assumed that *Jungle Hell* was its sole effort, and that the company was dissolved after losing in court.

Following that fiasco, Sabu was next contacted by producer Maurice Duke for another stab at a television series. This one was partially successful in that two episodes were filmed, but Duke could not interest any network or local stations into buying the idea. So the episodes were edited together to make a feature film which was released by Allied Artists in late 1957.

Sabu and the Magic Ring, as it was called, was supposedly based on tales from *The Arabian Nights*; the resulting travesty must have sent Sir Richard Burton spinning in his grave. The only resemblance the movie bore to the famed tales of fantasy was its setting and the presence of an *ifrit* (evil genie).

Here again, Sabu failed to escape from his image; the ad campaign for the film proclaimed him "The Elephant Boy of Samarkand" and his role was that of stable boy for the caliph of that city. While a tongue-in-cheek approach was adopted, it was not clever enough to raise this production above any of its fellows. The pressbook states that an entire Persian village was constructed in a desert near Hollywood. If that is true, then it was largely wasted effort, as no desert footage is seen at any time during the proceedings. The building material bears scrutiny as well. In one scene, Sabu dodges a bandit about to head-butt him; the man collides with a "granite" block instead, leaving an impressive dent in the "stone". The costumes are either unimaginative or too imaginative, depending on one's viewpoint. They look like they were pulled off the rack in a thrift shop - during a power outage. The plot concerns the power-hungry wazir of Samarkand, who, while slowly poisoning the caliph, also finds time to chase stable boy Sabu, who has discovered the magic ring of King Solomon, with which he is able to summon a powerful *ifrit*. A goose swallows the ring, which results in a good bit of chasing about the marketplace. Once the goose's goose was got, Sabu, rearmed with the ring, en-

Sabu and the Magic Ring (Allied Artists, 1957)
Unknown actor, Sabu, unknown actor

ters the palace disguised as a prince so that he can inform the caliph of the wazir's plot. Ubal gives the caliph an antidote to the poison, and the wazir and his minions are defeated and made to disappear. The ring is then given to the *ifrit* with the admonition he find a deserving party upon whom to bestow it.

William Marshall (1924-2003) as Ubal the *ifrit* steals what there is of the picture. When asked by Sabu if he is a genie, he replies: "I am an *ifrit*; I eat genies for breakfast!" (Rex Ingram, take note!) At another point, he refers to a "standard book of regulations" for genies and *ifrits*. Even his magical powers cannot save this misbegotten movie; its television origins are all too apparent, from the lackluster direction to the shoddy sets and the uninspired storyline.

Back on the home front, no *ifrit* could have given Sabu and Marilyn a greater gift that year than what occurred on March 22 with the birth of their second child, a beautiful five-pound, eight-ounce baby girl christened Jasmine. It can truly be said: "Her eyes are Babylonian eyes." Her debt to the Sabu legacy was amply repaid in 1996 when she continued the adventures of Abu the Thief in a work of fantasy entitled *The Adventures of the Thief of Bagdad - Moonshadow*.

So much of the usual type of hokum continued to be sent to Sabu that he clearly wondered if he would ever be given an opportunity to grow as an actor. Due to his small stature of 5'6" (he had grown two inches while in the service), and no doubt also to his ethnicity, he was still considered a boy when films were being cast, even though he was now in his mid-thirties.

For well over a year Sabu rejected offer after offer, until one arrived from an unexpected source. Former actor and longtime director William Dieterle (1893-1972) contacted him through the William Morris Agency from his homeland of Germany, whence he had returned after a long career in Hollywood. The role he offered was that of an Asian scientist; an adult role at last, with nary a jungle or a wild animal in sight! Leaping at this opportunity so far removed from his image, the actor was soon on his way to Berlin to appear in the two-part *Herrin Der Welt* (*Mistress of the World*).

Based partly on Joe May's eight-part serial *Die Herrin Der Welt* (1920), this 1959 release updated the action to the present and altered the settings from China and Africa to Sweden and Cambodia. Indicative of the changed world situation, the serial's fabled treasure of the Queen of Sheba became a gigantic energy source capable of replacing all the power stations on earth.

Sabu's character, a major role, is that of Dr. Lin-Chor, assistant to the discoverer of the energy source. When the nuclear physicist decides that his discovery is too dangerous to entrust to mankind, he and Dr. Lin-Chor head for a Buddhist monastery in Cambodia. Unbeknownst to them, they are being trailed by one Madame Latour, who is after the formula. When the scientists learn of her presence, the physicist gives his documents to Lin-Chor and allows himself to be captured by Madame Latour's henchmen in order to give Lin-Chor time to reach Cambodia and become a member of the Buddhist community.

After having his advances rebuffed by Latour, one of her gang kills her and goes looking for Lin-Chor. Tracking him to the monastery, he shoots him in cold blood after grabbing the documents. He himself dies shortly after, and the daughter of the physicist turns the formula over to the abbot of the monastery, as her father would have wished. This marked the first and only time that Sabu's character died on screen, so it was a real departure at least in that respect. He must also have experienced some *deja vu* when he rode a water buffalo in one scene. Originally shown in theaters in two parts totaling 190 minutes, *Mistress of the World* was later trimmed to a 107-minute feature. While in this case the production values are excellent, the color is muted and flat, although this may have been intentional. The action scenes are poorly handled; Dieterle seemed to have left his sense of style back in Hollywood. One of the more interesting aspects of this picture is the international cast, which included American Martha Hyer (b. 1924), Italian Gino Cervi (1901-1974), French actress Micheline Presle (b. 1922), and Germans Wolfgang Preiss (1910-2002) and Carl Lange (1909-1999). Film veteran Valery Inkijinoff

(1895-1973), a White Russian who had fled to France after appearing in Pudovkin's *Storm Over Asia* (1928), played the abbot of the Buddhist monastery.

For the monastery scenes, Sabu submitted to having his head shaved. Since those were among the last scenes filmed, the actor returned to California with a nearly bald-pate, thoroughly confusing and frightening little Jasmine, who was used to her father's normally thick black hair. *Mistress of the World* proved to be the second of two films which were not released in the United States (*Baghdad* being the first).

In early 1960, Sabu received his first official recognition from Hollywood when he was included among the initial group of celebrities to receive stars on the newly-created "Walk of Fame". The date was February 9, and over fifteen hundred show-business personalities were honored during the inaugural dedication of the now-famous landmark. Fittingly, it was placed only a few steps west of one of the last great movie palaces built in America, the Pantages Theater.

Jasmine's shock at her daddy's altered appearance was nothing compared to that suffered by the actor later that year. On the night of June 23, 1960, his

Sabu's star on the Walk of Fame

brother Shaik was fatally shot outside his home in Van Nuys by one of his former employees. The assailant, who had been a delivery boy at Shaik's furniture store, turned himself in to the authorities four hours after the incident. He told the police that his intention had been to rob the merchant, who was known to carry large sums of cash. The eighteen-year-old high-school senior said that he drove to Dastagir's house, saw lights on, and peered in a window. Moments later, Shaik appeared outside, the two struggled, and the gun went off three times. One shot went wild; one hit the youth in the wrist, and the third hit Shaik in the shoulder and continued downward into his chest, killing him. The would-be robber fled without taking any money. He was later given a jail term of from one to ten years for involuntary manslaughter. Sabu's brother, who had recently been divorced, was only 48 years old.

When Sabu was told the tragic news, he was so stunned that he could not talk to reporters. Shaik had been the only link to his childhood, and now he was gone. Sabu had no other blood relatives, but he did have Marilyn and his children, and with their love and support he survived this ordeal.

Sabu did no film work for the next three years. Instead, he chose to enjoy life. Among his favorite pursuits were horseback riding (a skill he had taught his children very early on); fishing and sail boating on the lake on his property; and an annual family trip to Oregon in quest of steelhead trout. Never having lost his love for speed, Sabu owned several race cars which competed at Riverside Race Track. When Paul was six, he was given a silver midget racer, which his father tinkered with to increase its speed. Marilyn's fear for her son's safety was realized one day when he and Sabu returned from a race looking sheepish. Paul showed her a broken front tooth. Assured that he was not hurt and that a new tooth would grow in, Marilyn hoped that this incident would curb Paul's yen for racing. She was disappointed there. Another skill which Sabu passed on to Paul and Jasmine was swimming.

Even without an income from acting, Sabu managed quite well with the revenue from his real estate holdings and his contracting business. His own home was mortgage-free, and in truth, his film career was now considered secondary. While he had taken over management of the furniture store after Shaik's death, he spent very little time there, preferring to be with Marilyn and his children. Having a healthy and happy family meant more to him than the starring role in any motion picture.

The call of the klieg lights proved irresistible, however, and a year later newspapers reported that both Sabu and former movie Tarzan Johnny Weissmuller were once more looking for work. Sabu was quoted as saying, "I've had a number of offers, but since my brother's death I haven't felt like doing anything. I can't explain it. I just feel alone." The actor went on to say, "...but of course I would like to return to acting. I'll probably do some pictures in Europe. There were thoughts of my doing a television series here based on Rudyard Kipling's *Jungle Book*. But the sponsor felt the expense was too great. The reason is this: To shoot animal episodes in this country - and shoot many of them - is a terrific expense. You can't do it with stock shots and make it realistic. We made a pilot film, but that's as far as we got."

By then Sabu was resigned to his "Elephant Boy" image, for he added: "In these days they're not making my kind of picture. I can still work in Europe because they remember me there. The trouble with Hollywood today is the producers don't believe themselves their pictures can make money. They don't have faith. Before they begin a movie, they want to know how many millions it will make."

The following year Sabu received an unusual request from Great Britain. The British version of the popular American television series *This Is Your Life* was preparing a show to honor pop singing great Cleo Laine (b. 1927) and asked him to make an appearance. Sabu must have been the surprise guest of the evening, for the reason for his presence was a very obscure moment in Miss Laine's life. At the age of twelve, she had appeared as an extra in *The Thief of Bagdad* in one of the scenes shot at Denham. It is not likely that her footage survived the editing, for after one day she was asked to leave for distracting Sabu with her giggling!

This brief guest shot on a program, which was aired on

October 23, 1962, was Sabu's only appearance on British television, although he had appeared on several American programs, once winning a television set on a game show.

Back home after his short trip, the actor began picking through the scripts which had arrived during his absence. One that particularly attracted him would have him play a Malaysian guide for big-game hunters Robert Mitchum (1917-1997) and British actor Jack Hawkins (1910-1973), two major stars of the time. Based on a novel by Alan Caillou, *Rampage*, the story concerns a combination leopard-tiger known as "the Enchantress", which is sought by a West German zoo director. He commissions a noted big-game trapper (Mitchum) to capture it. He is accompanied to Malaysia by a famed big-game hunter (Hawkins) and his mistress, played by Italian actress Elsa Martinelli (b. 1932). The trapper and the woman are attracted to each other, creating a conflict between the trapper and the hunter. In Malaysia they hire a band of trackers, headed by Talib (Sabu), who is

Rampage (Warner Bros., 1963) Robert Mitchum, Cely Carillo, Sabu

described as "...top drawer...who also speaks Thai." Impressed by the trapper, Talib constantly offers him his wife (Cely Carrillo) assuring him that it is all right: "Plenty for two. Is custom.", he states. So much for how to keep warm on those cool jungle nights!

The rivalry between the men continues even after the woman declares her love for the trapper; the hunter, being a poor loser, feels compelled to face the big cat single-handedly in a cave. He has to be rescued by the trapper, who then captures the animal. Back in Germany, there is further foolishness, resulting in the hunter being mauled to death and the big cat being shot.

The picture was partly filmed in a studio, while the San Diego Zoo was used for the German zoo, and Hilo, Hawaii, stood in for Malaysia. While filming at the last-named locale, the lone local television station ran *Elephant Boy* every night the film company was there. As a result, Sabu found himself mobbed by a whole new generation of young fans on his way to location every day. The press also made much of his "comeback", since it was his first film work in over three years.

Sabu's superior swimming ability came in handy during filming on Hilo. Cely Carrillo, the Philippine singer who played his wife, got caught in an eddy during a scene where she slips and falls into a river. Both Sabu and Robert Mitchum dove in, but the faster Indian reached her first and brought her safely back to shore.

Rampage boasted fine production values and a score by Elmer Bernstein, termed "memorable" by noted film historian Leonard Maltin, and featured a catchy title tune. Sabu, appearing heavier than usual, got his fair share of screen time in the middle third of the picture, where he gets to order around the trackers and gun boys. The animal sequences are excellently handled, with the capture of the Enchantress in a hillside cave by Mitchum being especially exciting, as he is accidentally caught in the same net with the beast. Sabu and his boys save him from becoming cat food by quickly binding the carnivore's legs together.

On the whole, *Rampage* is a well-made picture that holds the viewer's interest, despite rather weak dialogue. Reviewers were mostly very kind to Sabu; *Newsweek* commented: "Only one true arresting moment - the appearance of Sabu, the old jungle boy, now a thirty-nine-year-old man, who plays Mitchum's native bearer and translator." Leo Mishkin in *The New York Morning Telegraph* was even more enthused by Sabu's presence: "Among the more interesting features of the new movie...is the appearance of an actor in a small, featured role whose name at one time was a household word. If, that is, the household also kept an elephant around the place. The actor is Sabu, once known as the Elephant Boy..." He concluded his review by saying: "It's nice, however, to see Sabu back on the screen again. Even without the elephants." You cannot please everyone, though. Howard Thompson of *The New York*

Times noted the "absurd dialogue," and was less than thrilled by Sabu's appearance. "Sabu ('Elephant Boy') is back," he wrote, "if anybody cares, with a middle-aged grin and looking downright frowsy." He should have been in the net with the Enchantress.

As part of the film's promotion, the studio invited a contingent from the famed Explorers Club in New York City to attend the opening. Their reaction was not recorded.

Sabu, although given fourth billing, had every reason to feel hopeful after appearing in this color Warner Bros. release, for his character had been critical to the plot. Even before the release of *Rampage*, he received a film offer from the Walt Disney studio. His "comeback" seemed well on its way.

Chapter Fourteen
The End of the Rainbow

With renewed optimism, Sabu began work on his twenty-second feature film in the summer of 1963. For *A Tiger Walks*, as in *Rampage*, he received fourth billing. This time he was to support Brian Keith (1921-1997), Vera Miles (b. 1929) and British child actress Pamela Franklin (b. 1950). Also, as in *Rampage*, he played a character critical to the story.

The plot of this Walt Disney production is not difficult to follow. The truck carrying the tigers for a traveling circus loses a tire in a small rural town. While repairs are being made, one of the tigers escapes when taunted by its trainer. The latter goes after the animal with a shotgun which he does not know is empty, and is subsequently killed by the beast.

Word of the escaped cat spreads rapidly and causes a media event in the normally sleepy hamlet. The sheriff (Keith) leads a party of deputies and townsmen in search of the carnivore, but they are severely hampered by a dense fog. When they discover the trainer's body, all but one of the townsmen immediately quit the party. This is the start of the exposure of the characters of all involved, from the governor of the state down to the sheriff's adolescent daughter (Franklin). The latter is shown as sensitive and loving and is almost the only one aside from Ram Singh (Sabu) who exhibits any common sense.

The hunt continues as tiger sightings occur at various points in the vicinity. After the sheriff's daughter airs her views on television, misunderstandings occur, resulting in the governor's calling in the National Guard. A nationwide "Save That Tiger" campaign also begins, which borrows the tune from the old college football song "Hold That Tiger" for its anthem. It is led by teachers and kids' show hosts. Meanwhile, the tiger wisely continues to distance itself from all the nonsense occurring in the town. With the lifting of the fog, the hunt resumes. The crew of a National Guard helicopter spots the fleeing cat in the hills outside of the town and troops surround the area. They begin firing mortar rounds in an effort to drive the animal toward open ground. The sheriff, whose daughter has finally gotten across her conservationist views to him, attempts to get permission for Ram Singh to go after the cat with a net, but is overruled by the pompous governor. Ram Singh, knowing the tiger's habits, points out where it will most likely run, and he, with the sheriff and his chief deputy, circle around the soldiers to reach the spot. As they wait, the sheriff's children bring him a tranquilizer gun he had ordered from a nearby zoo. Just after they reach safety, the tiger appears. It leaps past the sheriff, who shoots it, but not before having his shoulder clawed. Ram Singh and the deputy toss nets over the tiger as it struggles against the sedative. All ends well as the sheriff, who had been running for re-election, wins, and the tiger and its family are transferred to a zoo, having been bought by the contributions to the "Save That Tiger" campaign.

Though competently directed and nicely photographed, *A Tiger Walks* did not make any "Ten Best" lists for 1964. Its unsavory depictions of adults in what is essentially a children's' film leave a rather bad taste. Furthermore, none seems to have learned anything from his or her experience by the end of the picture. From the greedy, opportunistic hotel owner to the hyperbole-prone governor, these "grown-ups" are anything but mature. Old-timers Frank McHugh (1898-1981), as the town garage owner/mechanic, and Una Merkel (1903-1986), as the hotel owner, added a nostalgic touch as well as their experience to the proceedings.   Sabu's character, as previously mentioned, is vital, though appearing in but nine scenes. As the only one familiar with the tiger's habits, he is indispensable to the sheriff, who is initially responsible for capturing the escaped animal. As in *Tangier,* he is off-screen for a lengthy stretch, but this time he returns for the climactic action scene.

While *A Tiger Walks* was being edited, Sabu received his third film proposal for the year in November. Besides a good salary, it offered the veteran actor an opportunity to travel to Spain, a country he had never visited. Sabu was able to enjoy a quiet Thanksgiving dinner with his wife and children - Paul, now twelve years old, and little Jasmine, only six years of age, before the family prepared for its trip. A few days later, the enthusiastic film star reported for the required physical examination and was told by the physician that if everyone were as healthy as he, there would be no need for doctors. Returning home in high spirits, he did not know that he had but two days more to live. On December 2, 1963, Sabu, *né* Selar Shaik, suffered a sudden fatal heart attack and died in the arms of his beloved Marilyn.

The funeral was held December 5 at the picturesque Chapel of the Hills in Forest Lawn Memorial Park. The Reverend Dr. Clair Gahagan of the First Presbyterian Church of Hollywood officiated. Originally a Muslim, Sabu had converted to the Methodist faith at an early age and was a member of the Hollywood Masonic Lodge at the time of his death.

Only a handful of people attended his funeral, on a day when late afternoon sunlight streamed through stained-glass windows. Marilyn, Paul and Jasmine joined hands at the base of the steps leading to the casket as the last hushed words were spoken. How quiet it was, and how far removed from the beat of a throbbing drum resounding over the mountaintops of a far-off Himalayan kingdom. How remote from the time a youthful figure slipped through the shadowed jungle night to come upon the moonlit monoliths of a long-forgotten city and the treasure it contained. How distant from the time the earth was new, and one could sail the waters of the great Euphrates singing a jaunty tune as the cloud-capped towers of fabled Basra swing suddenly into view.

Malcolm Willits was present at Sabu's funeral, taking it upon himself to represent the actor's many fans. Afterward he joined the cortege in his 1953 Nash Ambassador, keeping well in back of the slow-moving line of cars. Interment took place on the side of a hill with spacious lawns in every direction. In the distance, the city of Los Angeles pulsated in the daily task of creating itself anew. How far away was timeless India. The service was brief, and afterwards those who had loved Sabu made their way home quietly in the evening traffic.

Many letters of sympathy were received by the family from the film community, including Louella Parsons and Hedda Hopper, neither of whom had ever written a disparaging word about Sabu in their newspaper columns. Hopper also expressed her feelings on the news of Sabu's passing in her column of December 6: "The death of Sabu saddened me. I'll never forget the first time I saw him. I was walking down the Strand in London when around the corner came the largest elephant I'd ever seen, and on top this beautiful 14-year-old boy. We met again when he was playing in *Black Narcissus* with Deborah Kerr and Jean Simmons. Lately he had worked more in real estate than pictures, but never lost his sweetness."

President Lyndon Johnson, in office only ten days following the assassination of President John F. Kennedy, took the time to send Marilyn a warm personal letter. Condolences would have undoubtedly been sent by the Korda brothers, but, sadly, Alex had died in 1956 and Zoltan had passed on just five years later. His widow, Joan, a former actress, sent a card of sympathy, but Vincent, the lone surviving member of that highly talented trio, was not heard from, being in Britain, busily engaged in designing sets for yet another motion picture.

The sad news was devastating to all who had watched "The Elephant Boy" grow up on the silver screen in a series of entertaining motion pictures over a generation. Although most of Sabu's post-war films were less than classics, his presence, with that matchless smile and irresistible charm, made them at least palatable. Fittingly, what turned out to be his final scene on screen showed him behind a group of children, wearing a turban and smiling his incomparable smile.

A Tiger Walks was released some three months after Sabu's death and quickly disappeared. It is probably the least remembered of Walt Disney's live-action films, hardly a worthy finale for the career of a star whose canon included such milestones as *The Thief of Bagdad* and *Jungle Book*. *Variety*'s review of the picture stated: "...the film's center of comic and dramatic gravity is synthetic and childish. But most kids will probably get a boot out of it," while Bosley Crowther of *The New York Times* remarked "...it demonstrates clearly that children love animals more than politicians do." Neither one bothered to mention the picture's sole distinction, that of containing the final role of one of filmdom's most beloved personalities. It is ironic that one who so personified youth should have died before attaining middle age. Perhaps his untimely death was to insure that his image would remain one of the unspoiled youngster seen in his early films, those which created that image and which are today most fondly remembered.

No moviegoer can forget the diminutive, self-sufficient Toomai in *Elephant Boy*; the regal Prince Azim in *The Drum*; the mischievous, freedom-loving urchin Abu in *The Thief of Bagdad*; and Kipling's wild child Mowgli in *Jungle Book*. Had Sabu made no other films, his importance in motion picture history would still be great.

Sabu's is a legacy unique in the annals of film. He remains the first and most enduring Indian-born international movie star. He was the first foreign child to break the color barrier in English-language films; the first to attain stardom in the process; and the first non-adult to make his name in adventure pictures. The films of no other child star offered the thrills, atmosphere and artistry that Sabu's did. Only *Wee Willie Winkie* (1937) and *The Blue Bird* (1940) with Shirley Temple, and *Captains Courageous* (1937) with Freddie Bartholomew, came close. Most of all, he left an image of exuberant youthfulness, matched only by Mickey Rooney, with whom he was frequently compared. Sabu was a golden child in a golden era of Hollywood history whose light has shone across the years. Neither his like nor such a radiant era will ever be seen again.

To visualize the ever-youthful Sabu as a supporting actor in such productions as *Gandhi* (1982) or *A Passage to India* (1984), with gray hair, and possibly a slowed step, is rather difficult, but it would have been heartwarming to see his career continue and mature.

Sabu is one of the very few stars who started at the top, remained there for almost a decade, and then began what was probably an inevitable downward spiral. Try naming a movie star who did not first appear in minor roles or whose career did not originate on the legitimate stage or vaudeville, in radio, or even on television. Name one who was not first a war hero, such as Audie Murphy, or a sports hero like Johnny Weissmuller, or who was placed in starring roles more from connections than any evidence of talent. It is not easy. Sabu had everything against him: he did not even speak English, and yet he overcame all obstacles.

The real key to Sabu's durability was his believability, which was as much a part of his attractiveness as his good looks. Sabu was a fine natural actor. Unschooled in the dramatic arts, he portrayed the roles he was given in a manner that conveyed his belief in them. He never overplayed or underplayed a part. Granted, his roles were not the most complex, but they required a certain quality which Sabu undeniably possessed. Proof is how well it registered on screen. With his passing the world lost not only a gifted performer, but also a truly unique individual who was loved by millions, and who made us all believe that "Everything is possible when seen through the eyes of youth."

The Thief of Bagdad (London Films/
UA, 1940) Sabu as Abu

Filmography

(All release dates are U.S. release dates, except for the Indian and German films.)

Elephant Boy

London Films

Released April 23, 1937

80 minutes.

Directors: Robert Flaherty, Zoltan Korda Producer: Alexander Korda Screenplay: John Collier (based on "Toomai of the Elephants" from The Jungle Books by Rudyard Kipling) Photography: Osmond Borradaile Screenplay collaboration by: Akos Tolnay and Marcia DeSilva Supervising Editor: William Hornbeck Assistant Directors: David Flaherty, Geoffrey Boothby Musical Score: John Greenwood Musical Director: Muir Mathieson Recording Director: A.W. Watkins Film Editor: Charles Crichton Sound Recordist: H.G. Cape Production Assistant: Andre de Toth

CAST: Sabu (Toomai), Walter Hudd (Petersen), W.E.Holloway (Father), Allan Jeayes (Machua Appa), Bruce Gordon (Rham Lahl), D.J. Williams (Hunter), Hyde-White (later Wilfrid Hyde-White) (Commissioner), Dastagir Shaik.

The Drum (U.S.: Drums)

London Films

Released September 30, 1938

96 minutes. Technicolor.

Director: Zoltan Korda Producer: Alexander Korda Screenplay:
Arthur Wimperis, Patrick Kirwin, and Hugh Gray from Lajos
Biro's adaptation of the novel by A.E.W. Mason Photography:
Georges Perinal Exterior Photography: Osmond Borradaile
Camera Operator: Robert Krasker Color Technicians: Christo-
pher Challis and Geoffrey Unsworth Art Direction: Vincent Korda
and Ferdinand Bellan Music: John Greenwood and Miklos Rozsa
Musical Direction: Muir Mathieson Supervising Editor: William
Hornbeck Editor: Henry Cornelius Assistant Editor: Maurice
Harley Production Manager: David Cunynghame Production
Assistant: Andre de Toth Assistant Director: Geoffrey Boothby
Sound: A.W. Watkins Dresses designed by: René Hubert Indian
costumes by: Phil Gough Technicolor Photographic Advisor:
Aldo Ermine Technicolor Director: Natalie Kalmus Technical Ad-
visors: Brigadier Hector Campbell and Lt. Col. F.D. Henslowe

CAST: Sabu (Prince Azim), Roger Livesey (Capt. Carruthers), Ray-
mond Massey (Prince Ghul), Valerie Hobson (Mrs. Carruthers),
Desmond Tester (Bill Holder), Martin Walker (Herrick), David
Tree (Lt. Escot), Francis L. Sullivan (Governor), Roy Emerton
(Wafadar), Edward Lexy (Sgt-Major Kernel), Julien Mitchell
(Sergeant), Amid Toftazani (Mohammed Khan), Archibald Batty
(Major Bond), Frederick Culley (Dr. Murphy), Charles Oliver
(Rajab), Alf Goddard (Pvt. Kelly), Ronald Adam (Major Gregoff),
Lawrence Baskcomb (Zarrulah), Michael Martin Harvey (Mullah),
Miriam Pieris (Indian Dancer).

Author's note: Having exhausted all possibilities, I was unable to find
the name of the actor who played the Old Khan, Prince Azim's
father. Although it was a speaking part, it was not credited.

The Thief of Bagdad

Alexander Korda Films Released December 25, 1940 106 minutes. Technicolor.

Producer: Alexander Korda Directors: Ludwig Berger, Michael Powell, Tim Whelan (uncredited: Zoltan Korda, William Cameron Menzies, Alexander Korda) Associate Producers: Zoltan Korda, William Cameron Menzies Screenplay: Lajos Biro Adaptation/ Dialogue: Miles Malleson Photography: Georges Perinal Exterior Photography: Osmond Borradaile Camera Operator: Robert Krasker Special Effects Directed By: Lawrence Butler Optical Photographic Effects By: Tom Howard Assistant Directors: Geoffrey Boothby, Charles David Art Direction: Vincent Korda Assistant Art Directors: W. Percy Day, William Cameron Menzies, Frederick Pusey, Ferdinand Bellan Supervising Editor: William Hornbeck Editor: Charles Crichton Music and songs: Miklos Rozsa Songs: "I Want To Be A Sailor"; "Back From The Sea"; "Heart of Mine, Be Still Today", music by Miklos Rozsa, lyrics by Robert Denham (Sir Robert Vansittart) Matte Assistant: Peter Ellenshaw Musical Direction: Muir Mathieson Costumes: Oliver Messel, John Armstrong, Marcel Wertes

Sound: A.W. Watkins Technicolor Director: Natalie Kalmus

CAST: Conrad Veidt (Jaffar), Sabu (Abu), June Duprez (Princess), John Justin (Ahmad), Rex Ingram (Djinni), Mary Morris (Halima/ Silver Maid), Miles Malleson (Sultan of Basra), Morton Selten (Old King), Bruce Winston (Merchant), Hay Petrie (Astrologer), Roy Emerton (Jailer), Allan Jeayes (Storyteller), Adelaide Hall (Singer), John Salew (Fish Peddler), Robert Greig (Man of Basra), Mark Stone (Masrur), Hewy Hallatt, Bunty Kelley, Umphra Beg, Sighe Khaa, Miki Hood, Ben Williams, C. William Carlton-Crave, Frank Tickle, Viscount the dog.

Academy Awards: Cinematography(Color); Art Direction(Color); Special Effects. Nomination: Music (Original Score).

Jungle Book

Alexander Korda Films

Released April 3, 1942

109 minutes. Technicolor.

Director: Zoltan Korda Producer: Alexander Korda Screenplay: Laurence Stallings, adapted from *The Jungle Books* by Rudyard Kipling Photography: Lee Garmes, A.S.C. Technicolor Photographic Representative: W. Howard Greene Production Designer: Vincent Korda Music: Miklos Rozsa Art Direction: Jack Okey, J. MacMillan Johnson Editor: William Hornbeck Second Unit Director: Andre de Toth Assistant Director: Lowell Farrell Special Effects: Lawrence Butler Production Manager: Walter Mayo Interior Decoration: Julia Heron Production Assistant: Charles David Technicolor Direction: Natalie Kalmus Academy Award Nominations: Cinematography(Color); Art Direction (Color), Music (Music Score of a Dramatic or Comedy Film); Special Effects.

CAST: Sabu (Mowgli), Joseph Calleia (Buldeo), John Qualen (The Barber), Frank Puglia (The Pundit), Rosemary DeCamp (Messua), Patricia O'Rourke (Mahala), Ralph Byrd (Durga), John Mather (Rao), Faith Brook (English Woman), Noble Johnson (Subarah).

Arabian Nights

Universal

Released December 25, 1942

86 minutes. Technicolor.

Director: John Rawlins Producer: Walter Wanger Story and screenplay: Michael Hogan Additional Dialogue: True Boardman Photography: Milton Krasner, A.S.C. Photography Associates:

William V. Skall, A. S. C.; W. Howard Greene, A.S.C. Music: Frank Skinner Assistant Director: Fred Frank Production Designers: Jack Otterson; Alexander Golitzen Set Decorator: R.A. Gausman Associate Set Decorator: Ira S. Webb Editor: Philip Cahn Women's Costumes: Vera West Music Direction: Charles Previn Sound Direction: Bernard B. Brown Sound Technician: William Fox Technical Advisor: Jamiel Hasson Academy Award Nominations: Cinematography(Color); Art Direction/ Interior Decoration(Color); Sound Recording; Music (Music Score of a Dramatic or Comedy Film).

CAST: Sabu (Ali Ben Ali), Jon Hall (Haroun al Raschid), Maria Montez (Sherazade), Leif Erikson (Kamar), Billy Gilbert (Almad), Edgar Barrier (Nadan), Richard Lane (Corporal), Turhan Bey (Captain), John Qualen (Aladdin), Shemp Howard (Sinbad), Wee "Willie" Davis (Valda), Thomas Gomez (Hakim, the Slave Trader), Jeni Le Gon (Sherazade's Dresser), Robert Greig (Eunuch-Story Teller), Charles Coleman (Eunuch), Adia Kuznetzoff (Slaver), Emory Parnell (Harem Sentry), Harry Cording (Blacksmith), Robin Raymond (Slave Girl), Carmen D'Antonio, Virginia Engels, Nedra Sanders, Mary Moore, Veronika Patsky, Jean Trent, Frances Gladwin, Rosemarie Dempsey, Patsy Mace, Pat Sterling, June Haley (Harem Girls), Andre Charlot, Frank Lackteen, Anthony Blair, Robert Barron, Art Miles, Murdock MacQuarrie (Bidders), Elyse Knox (Duenna), Burnu Acquanetta (Ishya), Ernest Whitman (Nubian Slave), Eva Puig (Old Woman), Ken Christy (Provost Marshal), Johnnie Berkes (Blind Beggar), Cordell Hickman, Paul Clayton (Black Boys) Phyllis Forbes, Peggy Satterlee, Helen Pender, Eloise Hardt (Virgins), Alaine Brandes (Street Slave Girl), Jamiel Hasson, Crane Whitley, Charles Alvarado (Officers), Duke York (Archer), Mickey Simpson (Hangman), Amador Guiterrez, Ben Ayassa Wadrassi, Edward Marmolejo, Daniel Barone (Tumblers), Kermit Maynard (Soldier).

White Savage

Universal

Released April 23, 1943

75 minutes. Technicolor.

Director: Arthur Lubin Producer: George Waggner Screenplay: Richard Brooks Original Story: Peter Milne Photography: Lester White, A.S.C.; William Snyder, A.S.C. Music: Frank Skinner Music Direction: Charles Previn Art Directors: John B. Goodman, Robert Boyle Set Decorations: R.A. Gausman, Ira S. Webb Editor: Russell Schoengarth Makeup: Jack Pierce Costumes: Vera West Sound Director: Bernard B. Brown Sound Technician: Charles Carroll Dialogue Director: Joan Hathaway Technical Director: John Datu Assistant Director: Charles Gould Choreography: Lester Horton

CAST: Maria Montez (Tahia), Jon Hall (Kaloe), Sabu (Orano), Thomas Gomez (Sam Miller), Sidney Toler (Wong), Paul Guilfoyle (Erik), Turhan Bey (Tamara), Don Terry (Cris), Constance Purdy (Blossom), Al Kikune (Guard), Frederick Brunn (Sully), Pedro deCordoba (Candlemaker), Anthony Warde (Clark), Jim Mitchell, Bella Lewitzky (Specialty Dancers), John Harmon (Williams), Minerva Urecal, Kate Lawson (Native Women), Alex Montoya (Guard at pool), Pat McKee, Jack Kenney (Sailors in bar).

Screen Snapshots #5 (Series 23)

Columbia

Released December 17, 1943

9 minutes.

Produced and Directed by: Richard Staub

CAST: Sabu, Cesar Romero, Richard Quine, Gig Young, The Ritz Brothers, Jimmy Durante, George Raft, Xavier Cugat, Col.

Towman, Major Petersen, Marlene Dietrich, Constance Moore, George Jessel, James Ellison, Bill Henry, Leo Carillo, Chris Pin-Martin, Bronco Billy Anderson.

Cobra Woman

Universal

Released May 12, 1944

71 minutes. Technicolor.

Director: Robert Siodmak Producer: George Waggner Screenplay: Gene Lewis, Richard Brooks Story: W. Scott Darling Photography: George Robinson, A.S.C.; Howard Greene, A.S.C. Music: Edward Ward Art Directors: John B. Goodman, Alexander Golitzen Makeup: Jack Pierce Gowns: Vera West Special Effects: John Fulton Editor: Charles Maynard Sound: Joe Lapis Sound Dir.: Bernard B. Brown Dance Director: Paul Oscard Cobra Woman Dance choreographed by: Carmen D'Antonio

CAST: Maria Montez (Tollea/Nadja), Jon Hall (Ramu), Sabu (Kado), Lon Chaney, Jr.(Hava), Edgar Barrier (Martok), Mary Nash (The Queen), Lois Collier (Veeda), Samuel S. Hinds (Father Paul), Moroni Olsen (MacDonald), Robert Barron (Chief Guard), Vivian Austin, Beth Dean, Paulita Arvizer (Handmaidens), Fritz Leiber (Venreau), Belle Mitchell (Native Woman), John Bagni (Native), Dale Van Sickel, Eddie Parker, George Magrill (Guards), Thelma Joel (Lady-in-waiting), Fernando Alvarado (Boy).

Tangier

Universal

Released March 8, 1946

76 minutes.

Director: George Waggner Producer: Paul Malvern Written by: M.M.
Musselman, Monty F. Collins (based on a story by Alice D.G.
Miller) Photography: Woody Bredell Music: Milton Rosen Musical Direction: Milton Rosen Editor: Edward Curtis Art Directors:
John B. Goodman, Sturges D. Carne Set Decoration: Russell A.
Gausman, Ted Von Hemert Costumes: Travis Banton Choreography: Lester Horton Music/lyrics: "Love Me Tonight": George
Waggner, Gabriel Ruiz, Jose Antonio Zorrill

CAST: Maria Montez (Rita), Robert Paige (Paul Kenyon), Sabu (Pepe),
Preston Foster (Col. Jose Artiego), Louise Allbritton (Dolores),
Kent Taylor (Ramon), J. Edward Bromberg (Alec Rocco), Reginald Denny (Fernandez), Charles Judels (Dmitri), Francis Mc-
Donald (Sanchez), Erno Verebes (Capt. Cartiaz), Peter George
Lynn (Lieutenant), Rebel Randell (Rocco's Girl), Dorothy Law-
rence (Maid), James Linn (Servant), Billy Greene (Mike), Phil Gar-
ris (Elevator Boy), John Banner (Ferris Wheel Operator), Charles
Wagenheim (Hadji), Joe Bernard, Dick Dickinson (Men), Charles
Stevens (Juan), Eddie Ryan, Jerry Riggio, Parker Garvie, Whea-
ton Chambers (Vendors), Billy Snyder (Barker), Margaret Hoff-
man (Police Matron), Jack Chefe (Hotel Clerk), Abel Pina, Henry
Pina, Jerry Pina, Jr., Antonio Pina (Tumbling Act), Bobby Barker
(Sergeant), Crystal White (Barber Maid), Murray Parker (Juggler),
Roxanne Hilton, Karen Raven (Girls), Pierre Andre, Maurice St.
Clair, Crystal White (Dance Doubles).

Screen Snapshots #7 (Series 25)

Columbia

Released March 15, 1946

9 minutes, 30 seconds.

<u>Produced and Directed by</u>: Richard Staub

<u>CAST</u>: Alan Mowbray, Victor Mature, Cesar Romero, Jerry Colonna, Tony Romano, Sabu, Frances Langford, Jon Hall, Kay Kyser, Ish Kabibble, The Hoosier Hotshots.

Black Narcissus

The Archers, for Independent Producers Ltd.

Released December 1947

100 minutes. Technicolor U.S. Distributor - Universal

<u>Directed and produced by</u>: Michael Powell and Emeric Pressburger <u>Screenplay</u>: Emeric Pressburger (based on the novel by Rumer Godden) <u>Associate Producer</u>: George P. Busby <u>Assistant Director</u>: Sydney Streeter <u>Photography</u>: Jack Cardiff <u>Camera Operators</u>: Chris Challis, Ted Scaife, Stan Sayer <u>Editor</u>: Reginald Mills <u>Production Designer</u>: Alfred Junge <u>Costumes</u>: Hein Heckroth <u>Music</u>: Brian Easdale <u>Music performed by</u>: London Symphony Orchestra <u>Assistant Art Director</u>: Arthur Lawson <u>Sound</u>: Stanley Lambourne <u>Process shots</u>: W. Percy Day <u>Technicolor Camera Assistant</u>.: Dick Allport <u>Makeup</u>: George Blackler <u>Assistant Makeup</u>: Ernest Gasser <u>Hair</u>: Biddy Chrystal <u>Assistant Hair</u>: June Robinson <u>Stills</u>: George Cannon(color), Max Rosher(b/w), Fred Daniels (portrait) <u>Color Control</u>: Natalie Kalmus <u>Associate</u>: Joan Bridge

<u>Academy Awards</u>: Cinematography(Color); Art Direction/Set Decoration (Color).

CAST: Deborah Kerr (Sister Clodagh), Sabu (The Young General), David Farrar (Mr. Dean), Flora Robson (Sister Philippa), Esmond Knight (The Old General), Kathleen Byron (Sister Ruth), Jenny Laird (Sister Honey), Judith Furse (Sister Briony), May Hallatt (Angu Ayah), Shaun Noble (Con), Eddie Whaley, Jr.(Joseph Antony), Nancy Roberts (Mother Dorothea), Jean Simmons (Kanchi), Phuba (Ley On).

The End of the River

The Archers

Released July 7, 1948

83 minutes (U.S.: 80 min.) U.S. Distributor: Universal-International

Director: Derek Twist Producers: Michael Powell and Emeric Pressburger Assistant Producer: George F. Busby Assistant Director: Geoffrey Lambert Screenplay: Wolfgang Wilhelm, from the novel by Desmond Holdridge Photography: Christopher Challis Music: Lambert Williamson Editor: Brereton Porter Production Manager: John Alderson Dubbing: Gordon K. McCallum Assistant Art Director: E.E.C. Scott Musical Direction: Muir Mathieson Sound: Charles Knott

CAST: Sabu (Manoel), Bibi Ferreira (Teresa), Esmond Knight (Dantos), Antoinette Cellier (Conceicao), Robert Douglas (Jones), Torin Thatcher (Lisboa), Orlando Martins (Harrigan), Raymond Lovell (Porpino), James Hayter (Chico), Nicolette Bernard (Dona Serafina), Minto Cato (Dona Paula), Maurice Denham (Defending Counsel), Eva Hudson (Maria Gonsalves), Alan Wheatley (Irygoyen), Charles Hawtrey (Raphael), Zena Marshall (Santa), Dennis Arundell (Continho), Milton Rosmer (The Judge), Peter Illing (Ship's Agent), Nino Rossini (Feliciano), Basil Appleby (Ship's Officer), Milo Sperber (Ze), Andrea Malandrinos (Officer of the Indian Protection Society), Arthur Goullet (The Pedlar), Russell Napier (The Padre), Thorn the dog.

Man-Eater of Kumaon

Monty Shaff Productions, Inc./Universal-International

Released July 22, 1948

79 minutes.

Director: Byron Haskin Producer: Monty Shaff, in association with
Frank P. Rosenberg Scenario: Jeanne Bartlett, Lewis Meltzer
Based on the book, *Man-eaters of Kumaon* by Jim Corbett
Adaptation by: Richard G. Hubler, Alden Nash Photography:
William C. Mellor, A.S.C. Music: Hans J. Salter Editor: George
Arthur Art Direction: Arthur Lonergin Set Decorations: Robert
Priestley Assistant. Director: Robert Agnew Production Supervi-
sor: Ben Hersh Dialogue Director: Joan Hathaway Second Unit
Director: Robert Tansey Makeup Artist: Robert Cowan Hair
Stylist: Ann Locker Sound: Franklin Hanson, Jr., Joseph I. Kane
Technical Advisor: Major M.H. Whyte, Indian Army, Retired

CAST: Sabu (Norain), Wendell Corey (Dr. John Collins), Joanna Page
(Lali), Morris Carnovsky (Gunga Ram), Argentina Brunetti (Sita),
James Moss (Panwah), Ted Hecht (Native Doctor), John Mans-
field (Bearer), Eddie Das (Ox-cart Driver), Charles Wagenheim
(Panwah's Father), Estelle Dodge (Mother), Lal Chand Mehra,
Phiroze Nazir, Virginia Wave (Farmers), Frank Lackteen, Jerry
Rizzio, Neyle Morrow, Alan Foster (Villagers), Ralph Moody (De-
serter), Edgar Barrier (Narrator).

Song of India

Columbia Released February 28, 1949 77 minutes.

Directed and produced by Albert S. Rogell Written by: Art Arthur and Kenneth Perkins (based on a story by Jerome Odlum) Associate Producer: Manning J. Post Photography: Henry Freulich, A.S.C. Music: Alexander Laszlo, based on N. Rimsky-Korsakov's *Song of India* Musical Director: M.W. Stoloff Editor: Charles Nelson Art Director: Sturges Carne Set Decorator: Sidney Clifford Assistant Director: Arthur S. Black Associate to Producer: Lee Frederic Sound Engineer: Jack Goodrich

CAST: Sabu (Ramdar), Gail Russell (Princess Tara), Turhan Bey (Gopal), Maharajah of Hakwar (Himself), Anthony Caruso (Major Doraj), Aminta Dyne (Aunt Shayla), Fritz Leiber (Nanaram), Trevor Bardette (Rewa), Robert H. Barrat (Maharajah of Ranjat, David Bond (Ranjit Singh), Rodric [Rodd] Redwing (Kumari), Ted Hecht (Numtai), Alex Montoya (Radio Aide), Al Kikune (Bearer), Edwin Max (Courier), Phil Nazir (First Herdsman), Ian MacDonald (Officer), George Bruggeman, Wanda Willis, Jack Del Rio, Delmar Costello, Rose Plummer (Villagers), Ethan Laidlaw, Marilyn Cooper (uncredited).

Savage Drums

Tom Productions/Lippert Pictures

Released June 22, 1951

70 minutes.

Produced and directed by: William Berke Executive Producer: Murray Lerner Screenplay: Fenton Earnshaw Assistant Director: Fritz Collings Camera: Jack Greenhaigh, A.S.C. Art Direction: F. Paul Sylos Editor: Carl Pierson, A.C.E. Set Decorator: Harry Reif Music: Darrell Calker Music Editor: Edward Haire Makeup: Paul

Stanhope <u>Wardrobe</u>: Al Berke <u>Script Supervisor:</u> Sam Freedle
<u>Special Effects</u>: Ben Southland <u>Optical Effects</u>: Ray Mercer,
A.S.C. <u>Sound</u>: Glen Glenn <u>Sound Editor</u>: Joe Evigan

<u>CAST</u>: Sabu (Tipo), Lita Baron (Sari), H.B. Warner (Maou), Sid Melton
(Jimmy), Stephen Geray (Borodoff), Bob Easton (Max), Margia
Dean (Tania), Francis Pierlot (Aruna), Paul Marion (Rata), Edward
Clark (Tahuana), Harold Fong (Officer), Rick Thompson (Spy),
John Mansfield (John), Ray Kinney (Rami).

Buongiorno, Elefante! (*Hello, Elphant!*)
(A.K.A. *Pardon My Trunk*; *Sabu, Prince Of Thieves*)

Produced by Rizzoli Film/Vittorio De Sica/Dear Film (Italy)

Released September 9, 1954

85 minutes.

<u>Director</u>: Gianni Franciolini <u>Screenplay</u>: Suso Cecchi D'Amico,
Cesare Zavattini <u>Director of Photography</u>: Anchise Brizzi, A.I.C.
<u>Editor:</u> Eraldo DaRoma <u>Assistant Editor:</u> Marcella Benvenuti
<u>Production Director</u>: Nino Misiano, A.D.C. <u>Music</u>: Alessandro
Cicognini <u>Assistant Directors</u>: Luisa Alessandri, Franco Monte-
murro <u>Art Director</u>: Piero Gherardi <u>Camera Operator</u>: Alberto
Fusi <u>Assistant Camera Operators</u>: Alfredo Palmieri, Ennio Guar-
nieri <u>Photographer</u>: Oscar DiSanto <u>Stills Photographer</u>: Angelo
Pennoni <u>Production Inspector</u>: Roberto Moretti <u>Production
Secretary</u>: Pasquale Misiano

<u>CAST</u>: Vittorio De Sica (the Teacher, Garetto), Maria Mercader (His
Wife), Sabu (the Indian Prince), Nando Bruno (the Landlord),
Gisella Sofio (Teacher's Girl Friend), Michele Sakara (Giovan-
nino), Ciro Berard (the Porter), Giuseppe Chinnici, Antonio
Nicotra (Doormen), Piero Mastrocinque, Pasquale DeFilippo,

Teresa Fimiani, Fausto Guerzoni (Tenants), Sonia Fort, Stefano Varretto, Giampiero Donini, Giuseppe Mendola (Garetto's children), Remo the elephant.

Baghdad
Falcon Films (India) Released 1954

Director: Nanabhai Bhatt Music: Bulo C. Rani

CAST: Bharati Devi, Ranjan, Anwar Hussein, Yashodhra Katju, Hari Shivdasani, Kamal, Bhagwan, Sabu.

Il Tesoro Del Bengala
(The Treasure Of Bengal)

Ferrania-Venturini Film/Specialty Pictures (Italy)

Released March 19, 1956

77 minutes. Color.

Director: Gianni Vernuccio Producer: Giorgio Venturini Screenplay: Piero deBernardi and Jean Paul Calligari, from a novel by Emilio Salgari Director of Photography: Renato Del Frate, A.I.C. Music: Italo Delle Case Conducted by: Gianni Vernuccio Photographer: Giovanni Costantini, Raffaele Del Monte Set Designer: Allemano Lowley Costume Designer: Maud Strudthoff Production Director: Leopoldo Imperiali Technical Director: Carlo Serrutini Editor: Loris Bellero Hair Dresser: Paolo Borselli Camera Operator: Antonio Gasparini Assistant Camera Operator: Giovanni Canovero Translator: Guglielmo Bonotti Assistant Translator: Romeo Fraticelli Assistant Director: Carla Ragionieri

CAST: Sabu (Ainar), Luisa Boni (Karima), Luigi Tosi (Don Fernando),

Ananda Koumar (Uzake), Georges Poujouly (Tomby), Carla Calo (Surama), Manuel Serrano (Burka), Nino Marchetti, Raf Pindi (Priest), Rita Caruso, Pamela Palma (Dancers), Lug the Leopard, Sacha the Tiger.

Jaguar

Republic

Released September 14, 1956

66 minutes.

Director: George Blair Associate Producers: Mickey Rooney and Maurice Duke Written by: John Fenton Murray and Benedict Freedman Director of Photography: Bud Thackery Art Director: Al Goodman Music: Van Alexander Assistant Director: Bart Carre Film Editor: Cliff Bell, A.C.E. Set Decoration: John McCarthy, Jr., and Otto Siegel Special Effects: Howard and Theodore Lydecker Makeup Supervision: Bob Mark Costume Supervision: Adele Palmer Sound: Melvin M. Metcalf, Sr. Optical Effects: Consolidated Film Industries

CAST: Sabu (Juano), Chiquita (Rita), Barton MacLane (Steve Bailey), Jonathan Hale (Dr. Powell), Touch (later Mike) Connors (Marty Lang), Jay Novello (Tupi), Fortunio Bonanova (Francisco Cervente), Nacho Galindo (Garcia Solimos), Redwing (First Porter), Pepe Hern (Jorge), Raymond Rosas (Motilon Boy), Frank Lackteen (First Priest), Dick Winslow (Second Priest), Charles Stevens (Campa).

The Black Panther

Howco Productions

Released December 26, 1956

26 minutes. Color.

Produced and directed by: Ron Ormond Screenplay: Orville Hampton Editor: Hugh Winn, A.C.E. Photography: Alan Stensvold, A.S.C. Assistant Director: Clark Paylow Makeup: Carlie Taylor Special Effects: Ray Mercer, A.S.C.

CAST: Sabu (Himself), Carol Varga (Ramee), Byron Keith (Maharaja), Nelson Leigh (High Priest), Don Harvey (Kurron), Jack Reitzen (Rajan), Rick Vallin (Kadlu).

Jungle Hell

Taj Mahal Productions, 1956 (not released theatrically due to lawsuit won by Sabu)

76 minutes.

Directed and produced by: Norman A. Cerf Executive Producer: J. Manning Post Story and screenplay: Norman A. Cerf Music: Nicholas Carras Assistant Director: Robert Vreeland Photography: Gilbert Warrenton Sound Recorder: Harry Mills Sound Effects: James Ekstadt Makeup: Harry Thomas

CAST: Sabu (The Jungle Boy), K.T. Stevens (Dr. Pamela Ames), David Bruce (Dr. Paul Morrison), George E. Stone (Mr. Trosk), Naji (Shan-Kar), Robert Cabal(Kumar), Serena Sande (Shusheila), Ted Stanhope (Dr. Angus Caldwell), Jacqueline Lacey (Secretary), Paul Dastagir (Child).

Sabu and the Magic Ring

Allied Artists

Released December 12, 1957

58 minutes. Color by DeLuxe.

Director: George Blair Producer: Maurice Duke Screenplay: Benedict
Freedman, John Fenton Murray, Sam Roeca. Based on stories
from *The Arabian Nights.* Associate Producer: Lonnie D'Orso As-
sistant Directors: Grayson Rogers, Ned Dobson Camera Opera-
tor: Archie Dalzell Art Director: David Milton Music: Marlin Skiles
Music Editor: Neil Brunnenkant Director of Photography: Harry
Newman, A.S.C. Film Editor: William Austin, A.C.E. Makeup:
John Holden Set Decoration: Hal Gossman Set Continuity: Gana
Jones Wardrobe: Bert Hendrikson, Sid Mintz Sound Recorder:
Ben Remington Sound Editor: Del Harris Recording Engineer:
Ralph Butler Special Effects: Augie Lohman Production Manager:
Allen K. Wood Construction Supervisor: James West Property:
Ted Mossman Sabu's costumes by: Eileen Younger

CAST: Sabu (Himself), William Marshall (Ubal), John Doucette (Kemel),
Peter Mamakos (Muzaffar), Daria Massey (Zumeela), Vladimir
Sokoloff (Ahmed Mirz, the Fakir), Robert Shafto (Caliph), George
Khoury (Phransigar), Robin Morse (Yunan), Bernard Rich (Ali), Ken-
neth Terrel, John Lomma (Soldiers), Cyril Delevanti (Abdul).

Herrin Der Welt
(*Mistress Of The World*)
(A.K.A. *Les Mysteres D'angkor, Il Mistero Dei Trei Continenti*)

CCC-Filmproduktion Artur Brauner, Berlin, in Co-production with Franco-London-Film, Paris, and Continental-Film, Rome/UFA-Film-verleih (Germany)

Released April 14, 1960

Eastmancolor.

Director: William Dieterle Producer: Helmut Ungerland Written by: Jo Eisinger and H.G. Peterrson Photography: Richard Angst Directors of Photography: Richard Oelers, Peter Homfield Editor: Jutta Hering (Part One); Ira Oberberg (Part Two) Music: Roman Vlad Costumes: Claudia Herberg Assistant Director: Roly Bock Art Direction: Willi Schatz and Helmut Nentwig

Shown in two parts - Part One 100 minutes, Part Two 90 minutes; later re-edited to a 107 minute feature.

CAST: Martha Hyer (Karin Johanson), Carlos Thompson (Peter Lundstrom), Micheline Presle (Madame Latour), Wolfgang Preiss (Dr. Brandes), Sabu (Dr. Lin-Chor), Lino Ventura (Biamonte), Hans Neilsen (Col. Dagget), Charles Regnier (Norvald), Carl Lange (Berakov), Leon Askin (Fernando), Rolf von Nauckhoff (Dalkin), Jean-Claude Michel (Ballard), Carlo Justini (Matrose Jean), Georges Riviere (Logan), Jochen Blume (Bertrand), Inkijinoff (Abt des Klosters), Gino Cervi (Prof. Johanson).

Rampage

Warner Brothers/Seven Arts/Talbot

Released October 12, 1963

98 minutes. Technicolor.

<u>Director:</u> Phil Karlson <u>Producer:</u> William Fadiman <u>Written by</u>: Robert Holt and Marguerite Roberts from the novel by Alan Caillou <u>Photography:</u> Harold Lipstein, A.S.C. <u>Art Direction:</u> Herman Blumenthal <u>Film Editor:</u> Gene Milford <u>Set Decoration:</u> George James Hopkins <u>Sound:</u> Stanley Jones <u>Assistant Director:</u> Clark Paylow <u>Second Unit Director:</u> Richard Talmadge <u>Makeup Supervisor:</u> Gordon Bau <u>Supervising Hair Stylist:</u> Jean Burt Reilly, C.H.S. <u>Music:</u> Elmer Bernstein <u>Song "Rampage":</u> Lyrics by Mack David, music by Elmer Bernstein <u>Associate Producer:</u> Thomas D. Tannenbaum <u>Production Supervisor:</u> Abe Steinberg <u>Animal Trainer:</u> Lutz Ruhe <u>Animal Handler:</u> Mel Koontz Miss Martinelli's clothes designed by Oleg Cassini.

<u>CAST:</u> Robert Mitchum (Harry Stanton), Jack Hawkins (Otto Abbott), Elsa Martinelli (Anna), Sabu (Talib), Cely Carrillo (Chep), Emile Genest (Karl Schelling), Stefan Schnabel (Sakai Chief), David Cadiente (Boka).

A Tiger Walks

Disney/Buena Vista

Released March 12, 1964

91 minutes. Technicolor.

Director: Norman Tokar Producers: Walt Disney, Bill Anderson Written by: Lowell S. Hawley (based on a novel by Ian Niall) Photography: William Snyder Music: Buddy Baker Musical Direction: Bob Brunner Editor: Grant K. Smith Art Direction: Carroll Clark, Marvin Aubrey Davis Set Decoration: Emile Kuri, Frank B. McKelvy Sound: Robert O. Cook Assistant Director: John C. Chulay Associate Producer: Ron Miller Costumes: Chuck Keehne, Gertrude Casey Music Editor: Evelyn Kennedy Makeup: Pat McNalley Hairstyling: La Rue Matheron

CAST: Brian Keith (Sheriff Pete Williams), Vera Miles (Dorothy Williams), Pamela Franklin (Julie Williams), Sabu (Ram Singh), Kevin Corcoran (Tom Hadley), Peter Brown (Vern Goodman), Edward Andrews (Governor), Una Merkel (Mrs. Watkins), Arthur Hunnicutt (Lewis), Connie Gilchrist (Mrs. Lewis), Theodore Marcuse (Josef Pietz), Merry Anders (Betty Collins), Frank McHugh (Bill Watkins), Doodles Weaver (Bob Evans), Jack Albertson (Sam Grant), Frank Aletter (Joe Riley), Donald May (Capt. Anderson), Robert Shayne (Governor's Advisor), Hal Peary (Uncle Harry), Ivor Francis (Mr.Wilson), Michael Fox, Richard O'Brien, Rajah the Bengal Tiger.

Bibliography

Allen, Jerry C. *Conrad Veidt - From Caligari To Casablanca* Boxwood Press, Pacific Palisades, CA 1993

Behlmer, Rudy - *Behind the Scenes, The Making of...* Samuel French, Hollywood 1990

Bernstein, Matthew - *Walter Wanger, Hollywood Independent* University of California Press Berkeley & Los Angeles 1994

Brosnan, John *Movie Magic* St. Martin's Press, New York 1974

Bucher, Felix *Screen Series - Germany* A. Zwemmer Ltd. London; A.S. Barnes & Co. New York 1970

Calder-Marshall, Arthur *The Innocent Eye: The Life Of Robert J. Flaherty* Harcourt, Brace, & World New York 1963

Cardiff, Jack *Magic Hour - The Life of a Cameraman* Faber and Faber, London & Boston 1996

Christie, Ian, ed. *Powell, Pressburger, and Others* British Film Institute, London 1978

——— *Arrows Of Desire* Waterstone & Co., Ltd. London 1985

Cohen, Morton, *Rudyard Kipling To Rider Haggard - The Record Of a Friendship* Hutchinson & Co., Ltd. London 1965

DeCamp, Rosemary *Tales From Hollywood* Cambria Spoken Words, Lomita, CA 1991

De Toth, Andre *Fragments - Portraits from the Inside* Faber and Faber, London & Boston 1994

Flaherty, Frances *Sabu The Elephant Boy* Oxford Univ. Press, NY 1937

—————— *Elephant Dance* Faber and Faber, London 1937

Godden, Rumer *Black Narcissus* Little, Brown, & Co., Boston 1939

Green, Roger L. *A. E. W. Mason* Parrish, London 1952

Griffith, Richard *The World Of Robert Flaherty* Duell, Sloan, & Pierce-Little, Brown Boston, New York 1953

Higham, Charles and Moseley, Roy *Princess Merle* Coward-McCann, Inc. New York 1983

Hirschhorn, Clive *The Universal Story* Crown Publishers, New York 1983

Huntley, John *British Technicolor Films* Skelton- Robinson, London 1949

Katz, Ephraim *The Film Encyclopedia,* fourth edition Harper Re-source, New York 2001

Kipling, Rudyard *The Jungle Books* The New American Library, Inc. New York 1961

Kobal, John - *People Will Talk* Alfred A. Knopf, New York 1985

Korda, Michael *Charmed Lives* Random House, NY 1979

Kulik, Carol *Alexander Korda: The Man Who Could Work Miracles* W.H. Allen, London 1975

Lady Kennet,Kathleen *Self-Portrait Of An Artist* John Murray, (Bruce) Young London 1949

McFarlane, Brian - *An Autobiography of British Cinema* Methuen, London 1997

Moorhouse, Geoffrey *India Brittanica* Harper & Row, NewYork 1983

Okuda, Ted *Grand National, Producers Releasing Corporation, and Screen Guild/Lippert* McFarland & Co., Jefferson, NC 1989

Parish, James Robert, and DeCarl, Lennard, *Hollywood Players: The Forties* Arlington House, New Rochelle, NY 1976

Parish, James Robert, and Stanke, Don E. *The Glamour Girls Arlington* House New Rochelle, NY 1975

Powell, Michael *A Life In Movies* Alfred A. Knopf, NY 1987

Rentschler, Eric, ed. *The Films Of G.W. Pabst - An Extraterritorial Cinema* Rutgers University Press New Brunswick and London 1990

Rotha, Paul *Robert J. Flaherty: A Biography* University of Pennsylvania Press Philadelphia 1983

Rozsa, Miklos *Double Life* Hippocrene Books New York 1982

Steinbrunner, Chris, and Goldblatt, Burt *Cinema of the Fantastic* Saturday Review Press, NY 1972

Stockham, Martin *The Korda Collection* Boxtree Ltd., London 1992

Thomas, Tony *The Great Adventure Films* Citadel Press Secaucus, NJ 1980

Walker, John, ed. *Halliwell's Filmgoer's and Video Viewer's Companion*, tenth ed. HarperCollins, New York 1993

Whittingham, Jack *Sabu of the Elephants* Hurst & Blackett, London 1938

Magazine Articles

Cinema Quarterly - Autumn 1933 "Alexander Korda and the International Film" interview with Stephen Watts

Film Comment - April 1987 "Great Balls of Fire" by Jim McDonough

Films in Review - November 1965 "Miklos Rozsa" by Ken Doeckel

Films in Review - October 1989 "Sabu" by Philip Leibfr[i]ed

Films in Review - March/April 1996 "Miklos Rozsa" by Bruce Eder

International Photographer - June 1941

Newspapers

The London Times

The Los Angeles Mirror

The Los Angeles Times

The New York Daily News

The New York Post

The New York Times

Variety

Website

Internet Movie Database – www.imdb.com

$\mathscr{I}ndex$

Some Comments From Those Who Knew Sabu

"His beautiful laughing face and his perfect athletic body were only exceeded by his courtesy and warm personality. For me he will always be riding off into the jungle lying between the giant horns of the water buffalo - a great star, but also a laughing lovable boy."

— Rosemary DeCamp (co-star, *Jungle Book*)

"...Sabu, as young as he was, was always most professional, most co-operative with all the actors, and above all a charming and intelligent young gentleman; it was a great pleasure to work with him."

— Robert Douglas (supporting actor, *The End of the River*)

"He was a naturally gentle, sweet, and uncomplicated person, very unlike some other movie stars I met during that summer. He had a good sense of humor. He loved American jokes and we laughed a lot."

— Lynne Lehrman Weiner (White Plains, New York)

"He made a great hit with the members of both the dramatic company and the choir because of his pleasing personality."

— Monroe Benton (Brewster, New York)

"We were so sad to hear of Sabu's death and also the tragedy of Shaik's death. They were lovely people - grand company, warm and generous."

— Mr. and Mrs. John D. Murphy (Merrick, New York)

"While working at Disney Publicity in New York, I was fortunate to meet many stars who would come to the New York office to publicize their films. One was Sabu, a very cooperative and fine gentleman. He would go around to each employee and introduce himself and shake hands with everyone."

— Philip Castanza (New York City, New York)

CPSIA information can be obtained at www.ICGtesting.com
Printed in the USA
LVOW072350120412

277384LV00019BA/114/P